LET'S EAT GRANDMA'S PILLS

ISBN 978-1-7353286-3-8   DWFC 234DEC31
Let's Eat Grandma's Pills

www.27bslash6.com

By the same author:

The Internet is a Playground
The *New York Times* bestselling book about missing cats, pie charts,
and badly drawn spiders.

I'll Go Home Then; It's Warm and Has Chairs
A book about floodlights, bad brochure design, and frozen mammoths.

Look Evelyn, Duck Dynasty Wiper Blades, We Should Get Them
A book about cabbages, beach cats, and pufferfish.

That's Not How You Wash a Squirrel
A book about toasted sandwiches, sociopathy, and secret tunnels.

Wrap It In a Bit of Cheese Like You're Tricking the Dog
A book about buttons, Polynesian island culture, and suggestion boxes.

Walk It Off, Princess
A book about cantilevers, Antarctic expeditions, and child care centres.

Burning Bridges to Light the Way
A book about sad parrots, dangerous frittatas, and poorly constructed bridges.

Sixteen Different Flavours of Hell
A book about paddleboards, telepathic cows, and tent pegs.

Deadlines Don't Care if Janet Doesn't Like Her Photo
A book about fish people, office romance, and big red rocks.

For Seb and Holly

Despite the fact they're dreadful.

Alternate Titles for This Book

Let's Poke Anemones

The Fence Fixing Wanderer

I'll Just Leave It Here, Under the Socks

Everybody Gets Punched

Book 3 of the Knifespawn Trilogy

Wig Money

Do You Have Any Quinoa?

A Bucket of Crabs

Shitholes I Hate and Am Never Going Back To

Slip Slop Slap

Bong Bing Bong Bong

Have I Mentioned My Bathmophobia?

Just Take Deep Breaths, Iris

It's an Hour Longer but There's No Tolls

Straight Snakes

Contents

Introduction

Where did the year go?

People say that even though they know where it went. Just because you had a blurry year doesn't mean the sequence of events that occur in an apparently irreversible succession from the past through to the present changed in any way. Clocks didn't get faster, you just didn't get out much.

This year did seem particularly blurry though, didn't it? Blurry is good I suppose, it means nothing memorably bad happened. It also means nothing memorably great happened though. The year probably wasn't as blurry for someone who found or lost someone, or won the lottery or went bankrupt, or travelled somewhere nice. Or maybe it's an unavoidable part of getting older; everything just gets blurrier until you die.

There were a couple of notable things that happened this year, things that would usually cause me to look back with a nod, but even those seem blurry now.

My offspring, Seb, moved out at some point this year. I can't remember exactly when even though it was a traumatic event for me at the time. I know not everything is about me, but it should be. Seb should have said to his tiny Asian girlfriend, "Sorry, I can't move in with you because that would mean dad will have to walk the dogs, mow the lawn, and take the trash out himself."

He still drops in occasionally, mainly just to poo, but never on Thursdays because that's when the trash goes out.

Agency-wise, Melissa, our office manager, had a baby this year. Its head is shaped like a squash and I refer to it as the squash baby. Not when Melissa's around obviously. I did refer to it as the squash baby in an email that Mike, our creative director, replied to and CC'd everyone on, but when Melissa demanded to know what I meant by it, I told her it's an Australian term for a baby you just want to hug so much you might squash it.

Melissa and her husband, Scoutmaster Andrew, named their new human Emily Elizabeth, after their mother's names, and, as their last name is Woodcock, this makes the baby's initials E.E.W. or 'eew'. Which is what I said the first time I saw a photo of it. It's not just me either, when Melissa sent us the photo, Mike's first statement was, "What's wrong with its head?"

I might actually draw a picture of it so you know what I'm talking about...

Okay, not an overly detailed drawing but the shape is spot on. Maybe it won't be quite as noticeable when eew grows hair. We had a temp in the office while Melissa was on maternity leave, which Melissa wasn't thrilled about. Whenever Melissa asked about her, I'd say, "She's pretty much the perfect employee. Everyone likes her a lot." The temp's name was Nadia and she wasn't the perfect employee. She was way too professional to be around people like us. For a while it made us step up, as if we needed to show her that we too were professional, but it was kind of exhausting and didn't last long. She left - after Mike attacked the photocopier with a hedge trimmer - citing 'unsafe environment' as her reason for leaving. Apparently a tiny piece of plastic hit her. Like we didn't all get hit by tiny pieces of plastic.

I also received my first formal complaint at work since Simon left several years ago. Gary, our accounts manager, filed the F26-A containing the single sentence, "David said my ears look like caterpillars."

Why would you file a complaint about that unless you knew there was truth to it? It illustrates the fact you can't discuss anything in the workplace without someone being offended these days.

In my defense, Gary's ears *are* astonishingly hairy - and I didn't actually say his ears look like caterpillars, I said it looked like he was wearing caterpillar earrings. I may have also stated that his ear hair adds three feet to his width and if he ever gets bored working at the agency he could find alternative employment at a carwash as one of the brushes. I don't just go around critiquing ear hair for no reason though; we were in a staff meeting and Gary kept asking people to speak up. It's like wearing sunglasses inside and complaining about how dark it is.

Most of the stuff that happened at the agency this year was blurry stuff. I went on a few business trips; Rebecca, our production manager, changed her hairstyle; Mike hurt his foot; Jodie, our senior designer, joined a community theatre group; and two of our designers, Walter and Ashley, moved in together.

Also, Ben, our copywriter, has a new girlfriend. They met on a dating site for people with autism. Ben doesn't have autism, but, in his words, "It's easy to fake, you just have to complain a lot and pretend to like ducks."

I should probably add that Kate, our HR manager, was a contestant on the local version of *Dancing With the Stars* this year. She's not a star by any stretch of the imagination but that didn't matter because nobody was. I don't even know why they called it *Dancing with the Stars*, it should have been called, *Dancing With People You've Never Heard Of.* The biggest star was a lady that owns a bakery. I originally had no intention of attending, but Kate told Holly about it and Holly bought a sparkly dress. You're not getting out of anything if your partner buys a sparkly dress. Kate and her dancing partner, an old guy named Dick, did an awkward tango comprising entirely of Dick clicking his fingers above his head while Kate walked around him for three minutes. I voted for someone else, I couldn't vote for that. At the end of Kate's dance, when the host asked a few contrived questions, Kate declared, "This has been a dream come true."

Pretty shitty dream. I had a dream about a talking mouse last week that was heaps better.

I also had to attend Jodie's community theatre group production of *Little Women*. It was in two parts and both parts went for two hours. I was so angry. The entire play was just four girls bitching about nothing. One writes a book and is sad because she has to edit it. Also, they eat a big breakfast and there's some stuff about apples.

Jodie asked me afterwards what I thought of the play and I told her I wouldn't have gone if I'd known it went for four hours and would rather be stabbed than ever have to sit through it again. Also, the costumes were shit. Don't ask if you don't want an honest opinion. It's not like I demanded a refund.

Usually Holly and I take a vacation somewhere each year, which defines certain years from other years, but we didn't travel at all during the Covid pandemic and have only taken a few short trips this year. Maybe that influenced the travel theme for this book. I think it was while I was stuck in a tunnel in Philadelphia with Holly and her parents for three hours and twelve minutes that I thought of writing a travel book titled, *Shitholes I Hate and Am Never Going Back To.* The title would have caused issues of course, I'd have to spell it as sh*tholes. I'm not sure why, perhaps certain people faint if they see the uncensored version. Regardless, it's not a very good title and this isn't a travel book.

I did stick with the travel theme for a solid twenty or so pages, but I'm easily distracted and occasionally wander off on tangents. Sometimes the tangents are longer than the original story and by the time I conclude the tangent, I can't remember what fat girls wearing Supreme® caps had to do with accommodation bookings. I'll usually just end the story at that point and hope that the reader got lost along the way as well.

For those disappointed that this isn't a travel book, and for those pretending to be disappointed because you don't have anything better to whine about, I've included ten handy travel tips below. If you specifically purchased this book just for travel tips, you could probably rip out this page, fold it, and call it a pocket-sized travel tip booklet:

1. If you tip your maid well, you can keep the sheets.

2. There's no time limit in the plane lavatory.

3. Remember to pack an adjustable spanner. You never know when you'll come across a really nice shower head.

4. That's semen on the remote control.

5. Heading to Denver? Why?

6. Bags of salt aren't a form of currency anywhere.

7. Caravanning? Don't forget Uno.

8. Forgot your phone charger? Rub your phone vigorously on the carpet for several minutes. It might work.

9. Pets? Put them down and buy new ones when you get back.

10. Whistling a chipper tune is worth seventy cents in Nebraska.

Bucket Lists

Hundreds of years ago, people didn't take quick trips to see the sights and buy a fridge magnet. Overseas travel meant booking passage on a ship and the voyage took months or even years. We're not talking Disney Cruiselines, there were no shows or shuffleboard, you just sat in a cabin hoping the ship didn't sink in a storm. Probably reading or cross-stitching on one of those things that looks like a cross between a little drum and a big homemade jam lid. If you were lucky enough to be on a ship that didn't sink, you died of scurvy unless someone remembered to pack grapefruit.

Even just seeing the other side of the country you lived in was a perilous undertaking. If you lived in the United Kingdom, highwaymen would jump out from behind trees and rob you of your belongings. Going anywhere in the United States meant buying a covered wagon and enough bonnets for everyone and, if you managed to avoid catching cholera or shitting yourself to death, there was a real chance of being trapped for the winter in a mountain pass and your travel companions eating you.

People in the 1800s didn't have 'parasailing in Bora Bora' on their bucket lists.

"I'm retiring, Reginald. Don't burn the candle too low, we're nigh out of tallow."
"I'll be up shortly, my dear, just compiling my bucket list."
"A list of buckets?"
"No, of places I'd like to see and things I'd like to do."
"Like what?"
"Well, I've heard the shire of Ashford has fifty cows. That would be a sight to behold."
"Ashford is over a hundred miles away, the perils of such a journey cannot be ignored."
"Yes, but fifty cows."

I was taught in school that the term 'kicking the bucket' originated in the dairy industry; that if a temperamental cow kicked over a bucket while it was being milked, the cow was sent to be butchered. It makes sense, but it's also wrong. It was my 4th grade history teacher, Mr Collins, who related the cow version, so who knows how many other falsehoods we were taught. I'm not saying he made things up, but I guess he taught what he was taught and facts got skewed along the way like Chinese Whispers. For years I thought a magic melon discovered turmeric until I relayed the fact to my sister and she said, "What the fuck is a magic melon? Do you mean Magellan?"

The term 'kicking the bucket' actually originated from a report of suicide published in *Jackson's Oxford Journal* of 27th September 1788, which states:

Last week John Marshfield, a labouring man, hanged himself in an out-house in Avon Street. He had very deliberately just before bought a piece of cord, which he put round his neck, and by standing on a bucket, fixed it to the beam. He then kicked the bucket a considerable distance from under him and was found soon after with his head almost severed from his body, owing to the smallness of the cord.

Which means a bucket list is technically a list of things to see and do before you hang yourself in a toilet. I discovered quite a bit about John Marshfield while I was researching the term's origin. It's surprising how deep links can take you; one minute you're researching someone's age, and the next you're an expert on thatch roofing.

According to historical records, John Marshfield was only 23 when he hanged himself. I get that 23 was probably the equivalent of today's 36, but it still seems young to be making such a permanent decision. My offspring, Seb, is 23 and the only decisions he makes involve Netflix. John worked as a labourer, mainly digging trenches and carrying building supplies, but had a side gig painting portraits. Apparently he was quite talented, but not enough so to make a living from it. It was unrequited love, as often seems the case, that drove John to end his life; a seamstress named Margaret chose a wealthier suitor to marry; a man named Edmund Plum who owned a thatch-based roofing business. Interestingly, Margaret and Edmund were later 'lost at sea' during a voyage to Portugal.

John was born on the same street where he died, which may have been common back then, but it may also indicate he didn't travel much. He also died in debt, owing £38 (about 5K in today's money) in court fines for setting fire to a fence. As such, it's unlikely he'd have been able to afford to go anywhere nice even if he wanted to. He couldn't even afford thick cord.

I wasn't able to discover why he set fire to a fence, perhaps it was Margaret's. We've all done stupid things in the name of love. I once mailed an ex-girlfriend a box with a poo in it. Regardless, I doubt the last thing John Marshfield thought before he kicked away the bucket was, "Didn't get to stay in a transparent bubble pod in Arizona, but fuck it."

Transparent Bubble Pods

There's no way I'd ever stay in a transparent bubble pod. Holly wants to stay in one but I'm not staying anywhere people can watch me sleeping. I've told her this several times but she still sends me links to 'immersive experience' getaways at least twice a week. I never open them because they always ask me to install an app. I'm not installing an app just to look at transparent bubble pods.

"Just install the app."
"No, I like a maximum of 24 apps so they don't go onto the next page. What was the link about? Is it another transparent bubble pod?"
"It's not a transparent bubble pod. It's a hollow log in a forest that you can spend the night in."
"Why would anyone want to spend the night in a log?"
"Wow, you really need to get out of your comfort zone. I'd love to spend a night in a log. One of the reviews says an anteater licked them."

I'm not a prima donna when it comes to accommodation but I do have three hotel room rules:

1. The room has to have a balcony so I have an escape route if the hotel catches fire. I'm not burning to death in a hotel. There's an average of 3,800 structural fires in hotels each year in the United States alone. I'm not really sure what it means by structural, I guess it's walls. I used to ask for extra sheets to ensure there were enough to construct a rope ladder from, but now I just pack my own rope.

2. There has to be a coffee maker in the room. A Starbucks next door or a pot in the foyer won't cut it, I need a coffee the moment I wake up, not after I've done my hair to go downstairs. I've considered taking my own Keurig machine and K-cups, but the rope takes up half my suitcase and I like to pack a lot of socks. Holly never packs enough socks and washes them in the sink. What's the point of having a nice hotel room if there's socks hanging everywhere to dry? We ordered room service once and when the guy wheeled the tray into our room, he said, "I'll just leave it here, under the socks." so it isn't just me.

3. The room has to have a king-sized bed. I'm not sharing a queen sized bed with Holly as she thrashes her arms about in her sleep like she's signalling a ship with semaphore flags. She also sweats a lot so it's like being slapped with fish.

Once we stayed in a room with two doubles, which I was initially pleased about, but Holly declared the second bed was the suitcase bed and made me share my bed with her.

"Okay, but you have to sleep with your arms pointing away from me."
"You're not the boss of sleeping positions."
"My bed, my rules."

I don't care if the room has a view or not, there's only so much staring out the window I plan to do. If it's a self-parking hotel I prefer to have a view of the parking lot so I can keep an eye on things. We once had our vehicle broken into while we were staying in a beach hotel and they took our fold-up chairs. We had to sit on towels on the beach like unemployed people. I'm never going to Florida again; too many thieves and fat girls wearing Supreme® caps.

Stick & Poke Tattoos

Travel has always been expensive. In many ways it's an elitist activity, a privilege only for the privileged. I have seen people travelling on the cheap but they always look like they slept on a beach and smell like a bag of potatoes that has been forgotten in the back of a cupboard.

They aren't the kind of people who own 'The Bigger Carry-On' with built in charger from Away, they own saggy backpacks and mostly visit countries like India and Indonesia because they can get a bowl of pingtongpok and a stick-&-poke tattoo there for 12 cents.

"How was your trip, Darrell?"
"So spiritual. I bought this bead bracelet for 3 cents from a child with no legs. Also, I go by Anugrah now."
"You do?"
"Yes. It means divine blessing in Hindu."
"Does that mean you'll need a new passport?"
"No, don't be stupid. Can I crash on your couch for a week or two? You'll hardly notice me, I spend most of my time playing my tongue drum. Do you have any quinoa?"

Jetties

My travel complacency may, in part, stem from family vacations when I was young. We didn't fly anywhere, flying was for rich people, we drove our station wagon with a caravan hitched to the back. Most of our vacations involved jetties for some reason. We'd walk to the end of each jetty, ask, "How deep do you reckon it is here?" and walk back. Then we'd play Uno in the caravan. I'm sure we did other things but I've either forgotten them or blocked them out. I do vaguely remember my father urinating on my stomach after I was stung by a jellyfish, and my sister Leith being hit by a car. I think she was on a rental bike.

Our caravan was a 1967 Franklin Caravelle that my father purchased for $700 from a man with one arm. It was originally white with lots of rust, but my father painted it red. I think white is the standard colour for caravans - it probably keeps them cool in the sun or something - but if you're parked in a caravan park with hundreds of other caravans, a red caravan is easier to spot when you're making your way back from the toilet block or tuck shop.

At least that was my father's reasoning. At night, the caravan looked black and we were once hit by another caravan backing in late because they thought it was an empty spot.

The interior of the caravan was predominantly orange with green carpet and denim curtains. My mother sewed the curtains out of old jeans and the pockets were useful for keeping small things in, like can openers and Uno decks. There was a double bed at one end for my parents, a small kitchenette with a sink and pump-tap, and a dining table with bench seats that converted into a second smaller bed - which I had to share with Leith.

The caravan didn't have a bathroom, but there was a bucket under one of the bench seats for use as a toilet when we weren't staying somewhere with facilities. It was courteous for everyone to leave the caravan while the bucket was in use, unless it was raining, in which case the user had to hold a towel up in front of themselves for privacy.

As my father had painted over the name 'Caravelle', he renamed the caravan SOLITUDE with white vinyl stickers. It was an odd choice of name as there was no solitude in the caravan, it was the opposite of solitude. Wherever you sat or stood, you were staring at someone.

My cousin Susan came on vacation with us once and when she realised it was just jetties, Uno, and staring at each other, she cried and begged to go home. My father made her a bed in the back of the station wagon and she only came out to eat, frown, and use the bucket. I was kind of annoyed because I'd asked several times if I could sleep in the car and was told, "No, there isn't enough air in there for a whole night and you can't have a window down because night wasps will get in and lay eggs in your ears."

Also, the very first time we took the caravan on vacation, we lost most of the vinyl stickers to wind during the drive and it just left TUD. My father must have rubbed those three letters down harder than the others because when he tried to remove the T, it took the red paint off with it - meaning we still had the T, it was just jaggedy like it was made out of electricity.

My father eventually hand-painted the other letters back on but he wasn't much of a typographer and the kerning was terrible. People always fuck up the Os. At one point he repainted the caravan white, but, despite several coats, the red showed through and looked pink so he repainted it again with brown fence paint. The white paint must have been oil based, and the brown paint latex based, as the caravan ended up with a craquelure effect like a dried up lake bed. It was only like that for a few weeks though.

During the caravan's final fun-filled family escape, the bit that connects to the car finally gave out to rust while we were ascending a steep hill. The station wagon shunted forward, snapping our necks back, and the caravan (now known as Brown Beauty II) rolled backwards - picking up speed in a wobbly, ziz-zaggy run that had vehicles behind us veering off the road into fields to avoid.

The caravan made it almost to the bottom of the hill but took a sharp right, hit an embankment, and become airborne for about thirty feet. The suspension must have been as rusted out as the connecter bit because the caravan didn't bounce when it landed, it just went flat - like a ball of dough dropped onto a floor.

It was one of only three times I remember seeing my father cry. Crying was for hysterical women and homosexuals. The first time was when his brother, my uncle Rob, committed suicide. Rob jumped from the top of the Rundle Mall carpark after his wife, my auntie Ruth, declared herself a lesbian and moved in with a woman named Helen who owned a bee-keeping farm. We weren't allowed to have honey in the house after that. The last time I saw my father cry was when a crow pecked out a chunk of flesh from the top of his head. I wrote about that in another book so I won't repeat it here otherwise people will bitch about it on Amazon.

 **Meh**

Not his worst book but I took off four stars because he mentioned the time his dad got pecked by a crow again.

You might think I'm exaggerating, but someone once gave me one star because their copy was delivered in the same box as a bottle of shampoo that leaked. Another gave me one star because the book was stolen from their porch.

I'm fine with people giving me one star if they think a book I wrote was crap, most of them are, but how is it my fault if a package is stolen? Buy a Ring doorbell if you live in a shitty neighbourhood. Your package will still get stolen but you can post the video on the Ring app and an old lady named Janet will leave a comment about people having no respect for other people's property since they stopped teaching the Bible in schools.

As my family picked through the wreckage and loaded what was salvageable into the back of our station wagon, my mother consoled my father by stating the caravan could be replaced. My father replied that he wasn't upset about the caravan, he hated it; he was upset because he knew how much my sister and I loved the family getaways. Which is probably a testament to our skill at disguising our true feelings to avoid disappointing him. It wasn't altruism, it was self-preservation.

"The town we're going to has the 7th longest jetty in Australia. I know you love jetties. Are you excited?"

"Um, yes."

"You don't sound excited. We're only going for you, you know. I don't give a fuck about jetties. I'd rather stay home and watch the cricket. I didn't even want kids, I wanted to be an actor. Thanks for ruining the vacation, David. Did I mention the town we're going to also has a lighthouse?"

"Can we go in the lighthouse?"

"No, but we can look at it from behind a fence."

My father did actually have a brief acting career before he met my mother. He was on a children's television show called *The Terrific Adventures of the Terrible Ten* - it aired sometime during the 60s. He was only in one episode, for about two seconds, but it was a speaking role. He banged on a window and yelled, "The town hall is on fire!"

He was also on the news once. A Channel 9 News crew was doing a story about petrol-pump prices spiking over the Easter weekend, and my father was filling up our station wagon at the time. He was asked if the price hikes affected him and he replied, "Yes, because I've got an 18-gallon tank." He rang my mother and told her to tape it, but she taped the Channel 7 News instead. They had a fight about it and he accused her of doing it on purpose because she was jealous.

And yes, I realize I sound like an ungrateful brat who should be thankful I had the type of parents who took me places and not the type that chains you in a basement. I'm not going to pretend that I have fond jetty memories though. A kid at my school named Carter had foster parents who took him to Bali. They stayed in a resort with a Kid's Club and he made a monkey out of coconut shells. He brought it to school for show & tell and it was actually pretty good. The only souvenir I remember getting on vacation was a t-shirt with a picture of a lighthouse on it. I had to make stuff up for show & tell.

"This is a dinner plate from the Titanic."
"Really David? It looks like a normal everyday plate."
"Yes, but if you lick it, it's salty."

It's not as if my show & tell items were the worst ones though. One of the kids in my class, a heifer named Louise, brought a different stick to show each week. There was nothing special about the sticks but she came up with a unique description and use for each.

"This is a brown furry stick. It's 72 centimetres long and looks a bit like a snake. You could use it to stir paint with without having to bend over much."
"It's very similar to the last stick you showed us, Louise."
"No, this one is longer."

I've gotten in trouble for using the term heifer before so I should probably come up with an alternative. I say trouble but really it was just a few people emailing me to tell me they found the term offensive. There was no actual punishment. I'm not sure what the politically correct way of describing someone as fat is, maybe 'pleasantly plump'? Really, the only person who has the right to be offended by the term is the person being referred to as a heifer, and Louise doesn't care. She died in grade 9 from some kind of lymph node cancer.

We never did replace the caravan, which I was okay with, and after my father ran off with the lady who did the game scheduling at my parent's tennis club, there were no more family vacations. The only place Leith and I visited after my father left was our Auntie Phyllis' house. We stayed there for a week after my mother overdosed on sleeping pills - which hardly counts as a vacation as Phyllis made us tile and caulk her bathroom. My mother was fine, there was some stuff with child protection services but we got free grocery vouchers out of it.

I didn't even fly in a plane until I was 23 and that was just to be a witness in court proceedings against my grandfather for inappropriate behaviour towards Leith when she was eight. Which probably sounds worse than it was; it was mostly just about sunscreen application.

Sunscreen Application

"It happened seventeen years ago, Leith. What's the point of dredging it up now?"

"Time doesn't always heal wounds, sometimes they fester the longer they're left untreated."

"Sure. I'm not sure how helpful my testimony would be though. He rubbed sunscreen on me too."

"Yes, but you didn't have to get naked and bend over."

"I just don't know how I feel about pointing at our grandfather in court and stating, "He rubbed sunscreen on my sister's buttocks but not mine.""

"So you won't do it?"

"I didn't say that. It's just that he's 92 now and will probably be dead soon. Maybe some things are just better left..."

"You get a free flight to Geraldton."

"Fine."

My grandparents lived a block from the beach in a small Western Australian town called Geraldton. It's one of those towns where everyone knows everyone, which makes grocery shopping annoying.

There's not a lot to do in Geraldton but the beaches are nice and rarely busy; most of the tourists are passing through on their way to Kalbarri, which has nicer beaches, or Monkey Mia to be sexually assaulted by dolphins.

I was born in Geraldton but my family moved to Perth, a four-hour drive away, when I was four. We drove to visit my grandparents for seasonal holidays and special occasions, but, as my father and mother worked full-time, Leith and I were sometimes put on a Greyhound bus to go to Geraldton for school semester breaks. I was six or seven the last time we caught the bus there - a few months before my family moved to South Australia - Leith was eight.

We had cousins that lived in Geraldton but, apart from Leoni who was my sister's age, they were older and did older kid stuff. Leith and I spent most of our time watching television or at the beach poking anemones in rock pools. Sometimes we'd wade in the surf but we never went deeper than our knees because our oldest cousin, Matthew, was killed by a shark while in waist deep. The shark bit off his stomach which I think is the worst place to be bitten. It made the front page of the *Geraldton Weekly*; the article stated the shark probably thought Matthew was a seal and to avoid using white boogie boards.

There's a train track that runs through Geraldton. It's on sand dunes between a road and a wooden boardwalk that leads to the beach. A curve in the track further along means freight trains have to reduce speed before they reach it. Local kids would jump onto the back of a train when it was at its slowest, ride it for about half a mile, then jump off and roll down a large sand hill before the train started picking up speed again. It was called dune jumping.

A few months before Matthew had his stomach bitten off, he and my other cousin, George, convinced me to dune jump with them. They were both in their teens, had done it "hundreds of times", and informed me that being too scared to do it meant I was gay. They'd said the same about taking a puff of a cigarette, taking a sip of warm beer, and swimming out to a buoy and back earlier that day. I was just happy to be included and, I suppose, eager to impress. I didn't have any friends to hang around with and Matthew and George were super cool. They wore really tight t-shirts with a packet of cigarettes tucked under a sleeve and had long curly hair.

I had no hair because I'd caught nits at school a few weeks before and my father shaved my head. We didn't own clippers, he actually rubbed shaving cream onto my head and used a razor. Leith called me Yul Brynner for a bit but I didn't know who Yul Brynner was so it didn't bother me. A girl at school said I looked like a soldier which I was quite pleased about; I spent the day saluting people until a teacher told me stop. Also, I wasn't the only one at school with their head shaved, there'd been a bit of a nit pandemic and several other parents had also been too embarrassed to buy a bottle of Nonits® from a pharmacy.

"Do we have to shave it all off?"
"Yes, I'm not walking into a pharmacy and buying a bottle of Nonits® just because you decided to rub your head on some other kid's head."
"I didn't rub my head on anyone's head."
"Well you must have, that's how you get nits."

Grabbing onto the back of the train and pulling myself up onto the metal grill wasn't an issue; the train slowed to a jogging speed as Matthew and George had said it would. I did lose my flip flops while climbing up, but I knew where they were and could walk back along the tracks to retrieve them afterwards. It was jumping off the train that was the issue.

The train picked up speed quickly as it passed the curve and the jump-off dune was a lot steeper than I expected. I watched George jump and tumble down the dune, Matthew followed. "Jump!" they yelled, but I couldn't.

It was too high and fast and there were bushes - the type that sticks up and looks pointy. Maybe the train would slow down again I thought. It didn't, it got faster. I sat down on the metal grill, wrapped my arms around a ladder, and cried.

I did get to see a bit of the local scenery; at one point the tracks veered away from the beach and cut through the outback. A family of kangaroos jumped beside the train for a stretch but eventually fell behind. It was a hot afternoon and the sun beat down, heating the metal grill and ladder. I was only wearing boardshorts. Occasionally I'd lean out to look ahead but dust and grit got in my eyes and dried my mouth. I waved a few times, hoping to attract the attention of the driver, but it was one of those really long freight trains, the kind you sometimes have to wait ages for at railway crossings and someone says, "How fucking long is this train?"

I'd seen a movie or television show, probably a western, where someone riding a train had uncoupled the carriage. It was an option, I thought, as the carriage I was on would roll to a stop and the train driver would have to stop to come back and get it. I was on the very last carriage so it would require making my way to the next one - where I was fairly positive there'd be a lever marked 'let go' or something similar.

The ladder was scorching and the carriage rocked more the higher I climbed, but I made it to the top. The wind swept my hair back and my mouth did that centrifugal NASA ride thing. The carriage was open at the top and full of coal. Coal is a lot sharper to crawl over than you'd think and, being black, absorbs a lot of heat. It cut and burned my hands, knees, and bare feet as I crawled. I also fell onto my stomach and side a couple of times from the rocking. Sobbing, with snot streaming like banners in the wind, I looked back to see how far I'd progressed and discovered it was less than ten feet; there was no way I was going to make it. I was angry and frustrated and yelled into the wind before retracing my way back to the ladder and climbing down. I was now cut and bruised and covered in coal dust.

I had a pet lizard when I was five, his name was Stumpy because he was a Stumpy-tailed lizard; a common lizard in the Australian outback. He lived in my bedroom in a glass aquarium - I assume it's still called an aquarium even it doesn't have fish in it - with sand and rocks and a house made out of a milk carton. Sometimes I'd talk to Stumpy and occasionally pick him up, but, for the most part, he just sat there doing nothing at all. Which is why I didn't notice when he died. I have no idea *when* he died, I just picked him up one day and he was really light and stiff - like a lizard carved out of balsa wood.

That was how I'd be found, I thought. The train would just keep travelling around Australia for years until one day someone discovered me and asked what I was doing on the train and, when I didn't answer, they'd realise I was just a dried-up husk boy.

Also, while it isn't relative the story, when Stumpy died, I knew my parents would say something along the lines of, "That's why you're not getting a dog, you can't even keep a lizard alive," so I didn't tell them. Each morning, for an entire school term, I'd move Stumpy into a different place in his aquarium to make it appear he was still alive. Usually looking the other way because his eyes had turned white. I also make a big deal of catching any bugs or moths in the house to 'give to Stumpy' and made sure his water bowl was always full. At the end of the school term, before Leith and I left on the bus to Geraldton for two weeks, I put Stumpy inside his milk carton house. When I returned, Stumpy was *on top* of the milk carton house. Puzzled by this, I reached in to pick Stumpy up, and he bit me. Clearly my mother had checked on Stumpy, discovered he was dead, and replaced him. I couldn't say anything, or my parents would know I knew he was dead before I left, and they didn't say anything. I did change Stumpy's name, to Stumpy 2, but I said it in a way that my parents wouldn't catch on - such as, "Gosh I'm thirsty, I might have some water, and take some to Stumpy 2."

Several years later, I admitted to my parents that Stumpy had died before I left and they said they knew nothing about it. I'm not sure if they forgot or were keeping up the pretence, but there was no reason to lie after so much time had passed, and replacing a Stumpy-tailed lizard wouldn't have been a simple, easily forgotten task. Maybe it *was* Stumpy all along. Maybe he was just a bit dehydrated and had gotten wet while I was away. Maybe Stumpy-tailed lizards are like those frogs that sit under dried mud for years until it rains. It seems pretty unlikely but I'm no expert on lizards. I've only ever owned one. Maybe two. Who knows at this point.

Hours passed before the train veered back towards the coast and I sobbed with relief when I saw the beach again. I'd spent most of the time singing the theme song to *Kimba the White Lion* and counting railway ties as they passed below the metal grill. I'd closed my eyes at one point and nodded off, but was startled awake when the train blew its horn. I couldn't be certain, but it felt as if the train was slowing. It was getting dark by then but I decided that if the train slowed enough, and I saw a decent dune, I was going to jump - regardless of how steep it was or how many bushes there were. After that, I'd just walk along the beach until I got back to Geraldton. I had no idea had far it was, or how long it would take, but it was a better option than becoming a husk boy.

I didn't have to jump though, the train stopped at the next town. The local police had been notified of my journey and a car was waiting for me. A female officer cleaned me up at the station and gave me a sandwich and a bottle of Fanta. She called me her 'little explorer' which was nice. Another officer called me a fucking idiot. I slept on a chair under a borrowed jacket until my grandfather arrived, around midnight, to collect me and drive me home.

I assumed I'd be in a lot of trouble, but it was Matthew and George who were punished. They had to apologise to me and wash my grandfather's car. I offered to help, as I felt responsible, but Matthew sprayed me with a hose. I think my grandfather was more concerned about my parents finding out about my train ride than angry, as he gave me ten dollars not to mention it to them. I bought a glow in the dark frisbee and a C3PO mask with the money.

I did eventually tell my mother but she just said, "That never happened, why would you lie about something like that?" She said the same thing when Leith eventually told her about having sunscreen rubbed on her bum. My grandfather was a respected member of the community, he wore a suit and hat everywhere and was a member of the local Rotary club. Besides, where was my grandmother when all this supposedly happened?

Probably in bed. I don't remember much of my grandmother as she only left her bed to eat meals, watch *The Muppets,* and change her colostomy bag. Her bowel had been removed due to cancer at some point and she was on a lot of medication. Mostly she just smiled and ate biscuits. Sometimes she cried and when Leith or I asked if she was okay, she'd reply, "I wanted to join the Women's Auxiliary Australian Air Force."

My grandfather became angry when she cried and would shout, "They wouldn't have accepted you, Gwen, you're too short!" Once he yelled, "Oh, just fucking die already!" Leith and I usually went anemone poking when that happened.

I know my grandmother was on a lot of medication because there were bottles of pills everywhere. There were bottles in the kitchen, in the bathroom, and dozens beside her bed. Most of the bottles were orange but one of the bottles was cobalt blue; those were her special pills, her 'happy pills'. Whenever my grandmother became flustered, complained, or showed moments of clarity, my grandfather would ask Leith or I to get Grandma's happy pills for her.

One afternoon, towards the end of our last stay in Geraldton, tired of wading and poking anemones, Leith and I sat in an old wooden rowing boat that had been long forgotten in the sand dunes. It was half covered by sand and the hull had rotted away. When I asked Leith, "What do you want to do?", she rummaged in her pocket and produced six happy pills.

"Let's eat Grandma's pills," she said.
"What for?" I asked.
'Because they'll make us happy."
"I'm already happy."
"No you're not."

I wasn't any happier after taking the pills. I didn't feel anything. Leith made us wigs out of seaweed and we played Tiddlywinks with small shells, but then I just sat in the boat staring at one of the planks. I'm not sure for how long. The boat had been repainted several times during its life and the paint was peeled, showing the grey, cracked wood below. The paint layers on the plank I was staring at - mostly white but with areas of faded blue and red - were shaped like a face. A little face with red lips. It became bigger as I stared it, as if it was getting closer, then smiled. I jerked back, startled, and turned to Leith to ask if she had seen it. She wasn't in the boat, she was doing cartwheels by the shoreline. I yelled her name and she waved, calling me over, but as I started to climb out of the boat, the little face asked, "Where are you going?"

"To play with my sister," I told the face.

"Don't go, "the face said, "stay here and play with me."

"No," I replied, "you're just old paint."

"I hate you," the face said, its smile disappearing.

"Why? Because I want to go and play?"

"No, because you won't say anything about what Grandpa does with your sister."

Leith and I spent the rest of the afternoon under a jetty. Partly because it was shady, and partly because we were hiding; Leith had walked into a beachside shop, grabbed two Calippo popsicles, and ran. I was convinced the police were looking for us so I scoffed mine down and buried the wrapper deep in the sand. I never went back to the boat. I didn't even glance at it as we walked back.

The next day, my grandfather went crabbing and returned mid-afternoon with a large bucket of live crabs. Most of them were blue but there were a few smaller orange crabs as well. I watched as he brought a large pot of water to boil, selected a crab, and dropped it in.

Boiling crabs to death might be a perfectly acceptable way to kill them, I don't know, I don't kill crabs, but, at the time, I found it horrifying. When I voiced this to my grandfather, he laughed and stated, "Crabs don't feel pain, here watch..."

Grabbing a crab from the bucket, from behind so it couldn't nip him, he proceeded to pull its legs off one by one until only the claws were left. He then placed the crab on the kitchen floor and chuckled as it attempted to crawl away using just it's claws. The crab actually made it a short distance before my grandfather picked it up and threw it into the pot.

"Don't forget your legs," he said, throwing them in too.

I have no idea if crabs feel pain or not. There's no way of asking them so you can't say for certain they don't. Even if you're 99.9 percent positive crabs don't feel pain - because you read it somewhere or saw something about it on a documentary you watched for thirty seconds while channel surfing - the 0.1% chance they do means there's no need to be a dickhead about it.

I grabbed the bucket of crabs and ran.

The beach was only a short distance from the house, and I ran as fast as I could, but the bucket was heavy and my grandfather was surprisingly quick for an old guy. He regularly played lawn bowls which, for American readers, is like a cross between Bocce Ball and a wake. I could hear him behind me; his flip-flops went flip flip flip flip flip as he closed the distance.

I made it past the road, across the railway tracks, and down the boardwalk steps onto the beach. It was the soft sand that let me down. I don't have sand-runner calves. Still, I was only twenty feet from the water when he caught me. He swung me around and shook me, ripped the bucket from hand.

"Give it back," I shouted.

"No," my grandfather sneered, he tapped the side of his head, "There's something wrong with you, you know that? Your brain is broken. That's why your parents send you to stay with us. They can't stand you. Nobody can."

He turned his back and began walking away.

"Give it back or I'll tell dad you rubbed sunscreen on Leith's bum."

My grandfather stopped and turned, "What did you say?"

"Give me the crabs or I'll tell dad you rubbed sunscreen on Leith's bum."

There was maybe ten feet between us but he closed the distance in a fraction of a second and punched me. I don't think I'd ever been punched before, there had been schoolyard scraps and dead arms, but never an adult's fist to the side of my head. I went down instantly. The world blurred, darkened, I was enveloped in a thick *whomp whomp whomp* sound. I remember hearing a seagull and feeling sand beneath my fingers, confused for a moment as to why I was on the beach. I raised my throbbing head and rested on my elbows - watched my grandfather making his way back up the beach with the bucket.

Halfway up the boardwalk steps, he stopped and turned to look back. He stood there for maybe a minute, weighing his options I guess, then made his way back to where I was lying on the sand. He didn't say anything, he just placed the bucket at my feet and walked off.

We'd made a deal and I kept my end of the bargain. Partly because the crabs had been saved, partly because I was now terrified of my grandfather, and partly because later that evening, after we had KFC for dinner, he gave Leith and I twenty dollars each. I bought a t-shirt with a picture of a lighthouse on it and had enough left over to rent a kayak for an hour. Leith spent her twenty dollars on a hat shaped like an octopus and a kaleidoscope.

The bucket of crabs was bought up in court but it was a confusing back and forth and was eventually stricken from the record.

'Why 17 years later, Mr Thorne? Why didn't you tell an adult about the alleged sunscreen incident at the time if you found it so inappropriate?"
"He gave me a bucket of crabs."

My cousin Leoni was also in court. She had a few things to add about sleepovers and soapy baths, so there's always more to a story than there first appears.

I only glanced at my grandfather once during the trial; when I was asked to point at him. He was smaller than I remembered, frail, there was nothing fearful about him. Maybe that's why Leith wanted her moment in court, to show, before he died, that she was wasn't afraid of him, that she was in control. I'm not really sure what the point was. Maybe it's different for girls than boys. There were times in my childhood I was 'technically' violated, but I've never felt the need for retribution.

When I was about nine, I had a conversation with an old guy on a bus about computers, and he suggested I get off at his stop to see his Apple II. He did have an Apple II and we played *Lode Runner*, but we also traced our penises onto a piece of paper with a pen. It was for a research paper or something. He might have been a professor. Apparently I did it wrong so he had to trace mine for me a couple of times. The trick is to pull the foreskin back so you have a more defined edge to trace, otherwise it just looks like a mushroom with a bump.

I think I was about fourteen when I recalled the incident and realized there probably wasn't a research paper, he just wanted to touch my penis. I wasn't angry, I just thought, "Lol, good trick." It wasn't *my* penis that been touched, it was *that* David's penis. That David from years before. That David that fell for tricks that *this* David wouldn't. Maybe it's some kind of coping mechanism, a form of dissociation and my brain *is* broken, but I don't care. Stuff happens then other stuff happens.

My grandfather was found guilty on two counts of 'sexual misconduct with a minor under his protection'. The judge took his age and health, and the fact my grandmother had died a few years before, into account. He didn't have to serve time in jail; I don't think that was ever on the table. He had a stroke in the shower three weeks later - which sounds like an innuendo, but isn't. I think my father attended his funeral - Leith and I weren't invited.

Also, while the prosecution did cover my flight from Adelaide to Geraldton, I had to catch a train back. I feel I should have been informed about this earlier as I wouldn't have gone if I'd known. It's a 44-hour journey. Some people prefer trains over planes, because they get to see more, but there's nothing to see between Geraldton and Adelaide. The region, known as The Nullarbor Plain, is flat and arid with maybe a bush every 500 miles. At 1700 miles, that's 3.4 bushes. It's like being in a cryogenic pod headed to another planet but something goes wrong and you're aware for the entire journey. This was before mobile phones were a thing, and there was limited reading material on board, so I went into a kind of delirious cycle of staring out the window, nodding off, then checking how much time had passed. Usually it was about twenty minutes.

Years later, even seeing those little trains that do a loop in shopping malls causes me to break out in a sweat. It's probably how Vietnam vets feel when they hear party poppers.

Twenty Things to Avoid While on Vacation

1. An old couple named Don and Becky who want to be best friends and have over a hundred photos of their grandchildren on their Consumer Cellular flip-phones. Each 12dpi photo will take eight seconds to load.

2. Being electrocuted while swimming. You wouldn't think this was a thing, would you? It is though, 2,830 people were electrocuted while swimming this year alone. That's a global number, so it's a lot less than were killed by falling off a ladder, but it's still pretty high. Apparently it's most common around boat docks, especially ones that have lights or those big metal racks that lift the boat out of the water. One issue with the ground wire and anyone swimming nearby is zapped. It's not a quick zap either, it's just keeps zapping and you drown while you're being zapped. It's like two horrific deaths in one. There's no way to really test for it either, apart from not being the first in or maybe throwing a bit of bread in and seeing if it sizzles. That might work.

3. Paddle boarding. It's just stupid.

4. Greek people. Honestly, they're just dreadful. Not only do they throw peaches at you, if their peach tree hangs over your fence and you pick a few peaches, they try to charge you for them. A dollar a peach isn't reasonable and I'm fairly sure there's some kind of law that says you can take fruit off a tree that's overhanging your property. I'm never going to Greece.

5. Camping. Apparently when women give birth, there's some kind of chemical released in the brain that blurs the whole event and makes them think pushing a human out of their body wasn't as horrific as they thought it would be. Camping must release the same kind of chemical. Once you're home and have had a shower and are in your comfy clothes and watching Netflix, the memory of all the lifting and carrying things fades away. As does the worst sleep you've had in years and the whole sitting around a fire staring at each other thing. Also, camping looks fun in L.L.Bean catalogues and you'll probably flip through a couple before your next camping trip and think, "I should buy a vest." I own five vests and have never worn any of them. Whenever I'm looking for a jacket in my wardrobe and I come across a vest, I think, "It's cold outside so something with sleeves would probably be better." Plus all my vests are too puffy.

6. Dehydration. Holly and I once went to Nevada during summer and neither of us could poo for two weeks.

7. Cruises. Remember that time everyone on a cruise ship got sick and they wouldn't let anyone off for three weeks? People had to eat rats to survive. My parents went on a cruise once and my mother caught Legionnaires disease from a contaminated spa filter. She ended up having to spend three weeks in hospital so my father sent my sister and I to stay with our Auntie Phyllis. We had to sand and stain her floorboards. Also, don't expect the onboard entertainment to be anyone you've ever heard of. It will be an old guy named Andrew who knows four magic tricks.

8. Putting your shoes on in the morning without checking them first. This is particularly important in Australia; a shake and tap isn't good enough, you need to use a can of hairspray and a lighter.

9. Hiking. It's just walking.

10. Fire pits. It doesn't matter if there's nobody else sitting at the fire pit, if you sit down, other people will show up. When they do, you can't just get up and leave, you have to wait it out a bit so it doesn't look like you're only leaving because they sat down. Once, when Holly and I were in Eleuthera in the Bahamas, a guy with a guitar sat down next to us and started playing *Wonder Wall*. I asked him to leave and he said, "You don't own the firepit."

11. Picking up baby javelinas. A javelina is kind of like a wild boar that lives in Arizona. The babies are cute but the moms are mean. One minute your all, "Aw, are you lost little guy?" and the next you're on your way to emergency with a towel wrapped around your leg to stem the bleeding.

12. Becoming a drug mule. I've never actually done this but I saw a television show once where a guy got caught with drugs in his bum and was sentenced to ten years in a Turkish prison. He had to share a room and a poo bucket with about thirty other guys. There's no way I could poo in a bucket with thirty guys watching. I'd just hold it in until I died.

13. Being abducted while backpacking across Europe and having your mouth sewed to someone's rectum. Actually, being abducted whatever the outcome wouldn't be good. Unless you were abducted by an old couple who just want you to set up their smart TV and give you a bag of money for your trouble. Or by kind aliens who give you a watch that can stop time. I'm writing this at work and just asked my coworker Ben what his 'best case abduction scenario' would be, and he answered, "Duct tape precut to thirty-inch strips, eight of them," so I think he misinterpreted the question. Gary, our account rep, stated he'd like to be abducted by another company where people don't ask stupid questions.

14. Getting badly sunburnt in Mexico. Trust me, you don't want to go to a Mexican hospital; everyone yells and old ladies try to sell you roses. Also, someone will steal your iPhone and a mean nurse with flappy arms will call you 'estúpido hombre langosta' which translates to 'stupid lobster man'.

15. England. Everyone's miserable and slightly damp. Also, there's nothing to eat. English people just eat the same three meals their entire lives. It's like all exploration of taste and texture ceased once they discovered mashed potatoes.

16. Josh Gad. You're probably thinking that it's unlikely you'd run across Josh Gad, but he spends most of his time hanging out in public places hoping someone will recognise him. If you do encounter Josh Gad, it's best to tell him he's your favorite actor and that you were really upset when the television show *1600 Penn* was cancelled because it was really funny and Josh was great in it. Failing to do so will result in Josh Gad fanning out his neck folds like a cobra and spitting venom in your eyes. Then, as you writhe on the ground, Josh will extend his lower jaw and slowly consume you.

17. Philadelphia. Everything in Philadelphia has a thin coating of something on it that smells and feels like dried pickle juice.

18. Staying with friends or relatives. It doesn't work out cheaper because you'll have to take them out to dinner to thank them for letting you stay at their house and the bill will be $457.80. Also, they're going to cook at least twice and you'll have to eat the food even if their kitchen cleaning habits are questionable and they own cats that they let jump up on the counter. Plus you'll run out of things to talk about by 7pm but they'll make you sit around their shitty fire pit listening to Bruce Springsteen until 10pm.

19. Immersive experience accommodation. I'm not just talking about transparent bubble pods, there's a place in Alice Springs where you can spend the night in a bat cave. I don't need an immersive experience with bats. I have nothing against bats, I think they're cute, but they look like they bite

20. Being bitten.

Try Not to Get Bitten

I don't really have a philosophy, I think it's okay to just wander through life finding interesting things until you die, but if I had to come up with one, *try not to get bitten* works. It covers most aspects of life and is sensible advice.

I actually hate it when people ask, "What's your philosophy in life?" They're not asking because they care about yours, they just want to tell you theirs.

"What's your philosophy in life, David."
"I don't know, try not to get bitten?"
"Hmm, interesting. Mine is to live your life by a compass, not a clock."
"Nobody asked."

I suspect most people get their philosophies from Facebook posts of sunsets with quotes over them. It should be a rule that you have to come up with your own. Rebecca, a coworker at the agency I work for, has the quote 'Live, laugh, love' above her desk. It's in a rustic frame with a twig glued to the top. You know the kind;

Hobby Lobby sells them to pleasantly plump women with dusty homes. They're in the aisle next to the tin roosters.

"Live, laugh, love, Rebecca?"
"Yes, it's my philosophy. That and dance like nobody is watching."
"They're not really yours though, are they? It's not as if you sat in a cave contemplating the meaning of life and decided 'live, laugh, love, and dance with abandon' pretty much covers it."
"I just liked the frame."

I've seen Rebecca dance, there's no abandon, she just bends her elbows and shakes her shoulders like she's pushing a wobbly wheelbarrow. Technically she is alive, but rarely laughs, and the love is conditional; it doesn't apply to people who catch the bus or men who wear shorts.

Fuck Philadelphia

I'd rather spend a week in Denver than a day in Philadelphia and I hate Denver so much that I'm slightly cross just from mentioning it. Holly just walked past my office and asked, "What are you cross about?" and when I answered, "Denver," she gave me a sympathetic nod. Mentioning Philadelphia doesn't make me cross, it's more of a nauseated feeling, like when you discover mold spots on bread or see a magnified photo of a tick.

Most cities have their good and bad points, but there's no point to Philadelphia. From its corrugated roads to its unbearable residents, the entire city is a dump. The only good thing to ever come out of Philadelphia is the cream cheese.

No, wait, I just Googled Philadelphia Cream Cheese and it isn't from Philadelphia; it was invented in New York in 1872 and got its name as part of a marketing strategy to associate the product with dairy farming - for which Philadelphia was known at the time. Philadelphia isn't known for dairy farming anymore; it's known for meat with cheese on it. How is that a thing? Anyone can stick cheese on meat. Burgers have cheese on them. What else does Philadelphia have to offer? A cracked bell? Who gives a fuck.

The only people who think highly of Philadelphia are the Philadelphians. It's like a bus load of village idiots high-fiving each other because their bus is the best bus.

"Philly versus everybody!"
"Yeah! Our bus has wheels!"

If you've never been to Philadelphia, you're probably thinking, "Oh, David, stop exaggerating, it can't possibly be as bad as you're making it out to be." It is though, it's dreadful. There's a tangible pointlessness that blankets the entire city like a dense fog. The fog doesn't thin as it moves outwards into the suburbs, it solidifies into the form of newly constructed 4-bedroom, 3-bath homes full of framed Hobby Lobby quotes and picture frames that hold five wedding photos. I've been to Philadelphia twice; the first time because I didn't know better, and the second time because Holly's brother lives in Philadelphia and turned fifty.

"Have fun. I'm not going."
"Yes you are. It's Marty's fiftieth birthday. We're all going."
"Who's we?"
"You, me, and my parents."

"In different cars though, right?"

"Why would we take two cars?"

"It's a five-hour drive. I can't spend five hours in a vehicle with your parents. I'd rather be dragged behind on a rope."

"It's all arranged."

"I didn't agree to the arrangement. If I have to listen to Tom repeat directions and Maria complain about voting machine tampering for five hours, I'll intentionally swerve into oncoming traffic."

"I'll drive then. You can sit in the back with Tom."

"Why would I sit in the back with Tom?"

"Because Maria gets car-sick unless she sits in the front."

"Every time you speak it gets worse. Let me get this straight, I either sit in the back with Tom for five hours, or drive with Maria in the passenger seat beside me?"

"Yes."

"I'm definitely not going then."

"Yes you are, it's a big event."

"It is? How many people will there be?"

"I don't know, maybe a hundred."

There were nine people at the birthday party. It was held in the backyard of a newly constructed 4-bedroom, 3-bath home in the suburbs with a framed 'Bless this mess' quote in the living room and another that said 'eat' in the kitchen, which would have made more sense in the dining room.

One of the guests was a retired refrigeration technician who had several anecdotes about refrigeration. There was a bucket of sand at the far corner of the backyard, designated the smoking area, so I grabbed a chair and sat there, looking across the dog poo strewn lawn at the other party goers standing in a circle discussing the price of freon.

There should be rules for throwing a party, a basic set that even Philadelphians can understand:

Rule 1 should be something about having alcohol at a party. Yes, guests are meant to bring a bottle or six-pack, but they're not all going to. You need to purchase more than one bottle of Kirkland Sauvignon blanc to go round.

Rule 2 should cover music. There needs to be some. Decent music, on a decent Bluetooth speaker. Playing the *Top Gun* soundtrack on your phone doesn't cut it, even if you did make a bass enhancer out of a Pringle's tube and placed it high on a window sill. Haven't we all heard *Danger Zone* enough? It was dreadful when it first came out and hasn't aged well in 36 years. It's almost as bad as *Footloose* or *Eye of the Tiger*. The only good thing about *Eye of the Tiger* is the music video and you should watch it now on Youtube. I'll wait... Did you watch it? Did you see the bit where they're walking down the street at night and the guy at the back has to dodge a pole? It's about a minute in. If you didn't bother watching the video then rule 3 specifically applies to you.

Rule 3 should be about participation. As the host, it's your responsibility to ensure everyone feels welcome and is having a good time. This involves engaging in friendly conversation, introducing people, and (see rule 1) topping up drinks. It does not involve going inside to watch television while everyone else stands outside learning the history of refrigeration. Nobody cares that the first commercial household refrigerator was produced by General Motors in 1911 and its first popular line was the Kelvinator.

"How is this a big event, Holly?"

"Turning fifty is a big event."

"You made it seem like the party was going to be a big event. I was expecting a tent and catering. A Stouffer's Lasagna and a box of Triscuits isn't catering."

"There's also a block of cheese. You like cheese."

"You said there was going to be a hundred people here."

"I said, *maybe* a hundred people. It was a guess."

"An astonishingly inaccurate guess. More of a lie really. I feel deceived. This is the saddest gathering I've ever been to and that includes a child's funeral. I basically spent five hours in a car with your parents for fridge facts."

Thirteen hours there and back actually. I rode in the back for the first hour of the trip there, but Tom kept showing me his new Android phone so I swapped with Holly. I own an iPhone and don't give a fuck about other phones. Oh, you have a USB-C port? Good for you, now back in the field and tend to the crops; if you don't reach quota this month, your hut will be set on fire.

Driving with Maria beside me wasn't much better; every time I glanced over at the passenger-side mirror, Maria thought I was staring at her and stared back at me. At one point, due to Philadelphia's crinkle-cut roads, her dentures popped out. It's possible I overreacted, but I'd never had denture spit on my arm before so wasn't aware of the protocol.

Maria sat in the back on the way home so it must have been as traumatic for her as it was for me. Tom took the passenger seat, which wasn't one of the arrangement options.

"I'll navigate. My phone has Google it Maps. Take I76 to I81, it's an hour longer but there's no tolls."
"I actually prefer the car's built-in navigation system, Tom."
"Nonsense, it's not as good as Google it maps. You should turn it off to save electricity."

"The navigation system doesn't use electricity. I mean, it does, but it's part of the vehicle's electrical system. Turning it off doesn't save money."

"Is this the off button?"

"That's the seat warmer button. It has a picture of a seat with heat waves emanating off it."

"They're heat waves? I thought they were arrows."

"They are arrows, wavy red ones coming out of a seat."

"Well there you go. Arrows. Take 176 to 181, it's an hour longer but there's no tolls."

I've mentioned Philadelphia's roads twice, but I'm not sure I got the point across of just how bad they are. War-torn villages in third-world countries have better roads. There's more potholes and lost hubcaps than actual road; driving anywhere compresses your spine by about three inches. I was 6'3" when we drove into Philadelphia and needed a cushion to see over the dashboard when we left.

I think I may have also broken a rib; sadly, it wasn't the kind that punctures your heart and kills you instantly.

Tom's directions took us not only through hundreds of side streets with fissure-sized potholes, but into a traffic jam in a tunnel under a river. There was no reception in the tunnel, so Tom started a game of *I Spy* and Holly cried.

"I spy, with my little eye, something beginning with T."

"Tunnel?"

"Yes, your turn, David."

"Okay, C."

"No, you have to say 'I spy'."

"Does it really matter, Tom?"

"Yes, it's called *I Spy*, not *Name a Letter*."

"I spy with my little eye, something beginning with C."

"Is it car?"

"Yes. Are you crying, Holly?"

"We've moved less than ten feet in an hour."

"You don't get to cry. You and your parents wanted to come here, I'm the only one who's allowed to cry."

We weren't completely without entertainment. At around the two-hour mark, the driver of the vehicle in front of us exited his car and took a dump. We held eye-contact while he wiped himself with a Chick-fil-A bag.

Waiting an indefinite period of time is different from waiting a set period of time. Even if the set period is several hours, it's easier. You know what you have to work with and can accommodate. If I'd known we'd be stuck in a tunnel without reception for three hours and twelve minutes, I would have packed travel scrabble and snacks, maybe downloaded a few albums to my phone instead of having them on a magic cloud. Or not gone obviously.

There are dozens of possible outcomes to spending a large amount of time with people in a closed environment without external stimulation, they all branch from a simple basis though: would you spend your time with those people if you weren't forced to?

I can generally put up with other people - ones I like - for about two hours. The time varies and is dependent on several factors that may seem random and are. Having to justify my actions is one.

I once left a party after only one beer because a guy was wearing a cape. I'm not talking about a superhero cape, that would have been a lot better, I'm talking about the velvet-lined kind people used to wear out and about in England before everyone decided it looked stupid and stopped. I have no idea why he was wearing a cape and I don't care; I'm not hanging around cape people. They're the same type of people who blend their own vape-oils and can name all the Hobbits.

"Interesting point, but don't forget Bibbitypop poured drinks from a large wooden ladle."
"I do believe you're correct. But that would mean..."
"Exactly. There must have been *two* large wooden ladles at the Feast of Merriment in Stickshire."
"So many levels."

Yes, I'm sure *Land of the Rings* is a decent read if you're into magic hats and ornery dwarfs, I just think it could do with a bit of a rewrite; maybe edit it down to 300 pages and add at least one robot.

"We could play *I Spy* again."

"No, you ruined that game I'm afraid, Tom. V for vehicle is the same as C for car. Wait, I do actually have one, I spy with my little eye, something beginning with A."

"Automobile."

"Good guess, but no, it was Another car."

"You can't use two words."

"I can if I hyphenate. Maybe one of us should walk to the end of the tunnel to find out what's happening. They can't just leave us here this long, it's inhumane. They should make a guy on a bicycle ride down the tunnel with a sign."

"Saying what?"

"I don't know, Tom, maybe *No Swimming* or *Bike for Sale.*"

"One that told us what's going on would be better."

"Yes, probably. How are you doing back there, Holly? Anything to add to the conversation apart from informing us for the eighteenth time that you wish you were dead?

"No."

It's standard operating procedure that whenever Holly and I are out with her parents, Holly becomes mute. Tom and Maria rarely have anything to say either, so it's like being with three pod people. Pod people that stare. Once, when I was cross about eating at Applebees, I refused to be the one who broke the silence and we sat staring at each other for 4 minutes and 22 seconds. I timed it on my watch. When the silence *was* finally broken, it was just Holly stating, "David's cross about eating at Applebees."

"Okay, that was six minutes of silence apart from Holly moaning. Surely four adults can come up with one topic of interest. Name one, Tom, any topic."

"Like what?"

"Anything."

"I'm reading a book at the moment."

"You are? What's it about?"

"Tanks."

"The type that contains liquid or soldiers?"

"Soldiers."

"Okay. Is it any good?"

"Not really."

"I didn't even know you were interested in tanks."

"I'm not."

"What about you, Maria? Read any good books lately?"

"No."

"Do you have a fun topic you'd like to discuss, Holly? Any opinion on tanks?"

"I wish I was dead."

"Yes, we all wish we were dead."

I would have happily read a book about tanks while stuck in the tunnel. I would have read anything. I read other people's bumper stickers, number plates, even the tire markings on the car next to us. For one excited moment I thought the vehicle user manual might be in the glovebox, but there was only a weird wheel nut and a Home Depot receipt in there. The receipt actually got a bit of use as we invented a game called *David reads a price and Holly guesses the item*.

"Incorrect, the $14.99 was for a pair of gardening gloves. That seems rather expensive for gardening gloves don't you think? What even happened to those? Okay... $8.25."

Around the three-hour mark, delirium had taken over. I'm not sure if it was a build-up of carbon monoxide in an enclosed space, or that the mind can only cope for so long without stimulation, but at one stage Maria was singing German Christmas carols while Holly listed off names of all the snakes she could remember.

"Sechs eierlegende gänse,"
"Rattlesnake,"
"Sieben schwimmende schwäne,"
"Green snake,"
"Acht Mägde melken Kühe"
"Straight snake,"

There was a small argument over whether 'straight snake' is an actual type of snake, but apparently Holly is an expert on snakes because she's seen the movie *Anaconda* twice.

Tom was no longer speaking because nobody wanted to play *I Spy* despite the fact that he'd thought of a *really* good one. I was coping surprisingly well; there'd been a moment where my mind snapped in on itself like a slap-bracelet and I spoke in tongues, but nobody seemed to notice.

There'd also been a moment where I considered leaving the car and walking off. Not to discover the cause of the traffic jam and return with information, but to simply leave my phone and wallet and walk away. I'd walk until I couldn't walk anymore, maybe do a few farm chores in exchange for food along the way, then build myself a log cabin deep in a forest somewhere.

I'd need a few supplies, like an axe and a book on building log cabins, so I would actually need my wallet. That would also save me having to do farm chores; I doubt it's all ponytailed farm ladies who lost their husband in a tractor accident saying, "Well, there's a fence that needs fixing, are you any good with a hammer?", there's probably also quite a bit of lifting involved. And poo.

"Hello farm lady, I was wandering past and thought I'd stop to ask if you have any chores you need doing in exchange for a meal?"

"Well, the cow shed could do with a really good poo-scraping."

"I'm more of a fence-fixing wanderer actually, you don't have any fences in disrepair?"

"No, just lots of poo."

"I'll be on my way then. Sorry to bother you."

I have actually worked on a farm before. It was more of an orchard than a farm but they did have chickens. I was twelve and the owners of the farm - family friends named the Andersons - offered me two-hundred dollars to pick fruit on their property for two weeks during school break.

Two-hundred dollars was a lot of money back then, especially to a twelve-year-old growing up in a rough neighbourhood. The neighbourhood wasn't rough in the same way that places like The Bronx or Salisbury are rough, there wasn't a lot of crime, but people could be pretty sarcastic about your clothing. Especially sneakers for some reason - kids at my school fell into one of three camps; those wearing white Adidas Romes, those wearing black Adidas Koln IIs, and those wearing Kmart specials. It was like being in a gang with only one membership criteria.

I had Dunlop Volley knockoffs that said 'Doing Laps' on the heel. They cost $9.99 - I remember the price because Peter Jackson (not the director) brought a Kmart catalogue to school to prove my claim that they had cost $29.99 was a lie.

Having two-hundred dollars meant I could buy a pair of Romes *and* Koln IIs if I wanted. I'd decided on the Romes though, as Emma Jenkins had Koln IIs and I envisioned a kind of Capulet and Montague situation developing. We had both been in a school production of *Romeo & Juliet* earlier that year and while neither of us had lead roles, we did have one scene together where 'lady on street' buys a pie from 'man selling pies'. I played 'man pulling cart of straw' but we were all on the same street.

The Andersons lived in Berri, a town in the Riverland region of South Australia, about a three-hour bus ride from Adelaide where I lived. Berri is known as the fruit growing capital of South Australia, mainly for its oranges, so I assumed I'd be picking oranges. I wasn't, I was picking cranberries. South Australia isn't known for its cranberries. It's a fussy fruit that likes a bog. The Andersons, however, having a low-lying area of their property that could be flooded, decided to give it a try; cranberries are expensive in Australia, most are imported, so a successful local yield would prove profitable.

Growing and harvesting cranberries is a bit of a process; the cranberries grow on low tangly vines and the only way to harvest them is to flood the area with water, causing the buoyant cranberries to float.

Cranberry pickers, wearing big rubber waders, then wade among the floating cranberries picking them. You may have seen the adverts for cranberries with two guys standing in a cranberry bog and wondered, what's going on there? Well, that's what's going on there. The one thing that's missing from those adverts is the spiders.

Cranberries are not only particular about the growing conditions, they also have an issue with pesticides. I don't know if it's because they absorb the pesticides or just don't like them, but they can't be sprayed with standard chemicals. As such, a natural alternative to pest control is used: wolf spiders. There's actually a market for wolf spider eggs and cranberry farms buy a lot of them. During each cranberry season, tens of thousands of wolf spiders make their home among the vines. They're happy enough until the bog is flooded at harvest time, at which time they seek the highest point out of the water: *the pickers.*

The first question people applying for cranberry picking jobs are usually asked is, "Do you have a problem with spiders?"

Nobody asked if I had a problem with spiders. It's possible the Andersons, being that it was their first cranberry crop, had no idea what was about to happen. Or perhaps they did but didn't bother asking because everyone in Australia has a problem with spiders. Everything in Australia that's not a spider has a spider on it, in it, or under it. We have spiders the size of small children that chase you on hiking trails; they live in holes with a secret door and know to wait until you're several steps past them and looking the other way before they run out and wrap themselves around your leg.

"American?"

"Yes, we're visiting for the week. Planning to take in a few hiking trails."

"Nice. Do you own kevlar pants?"

"No, will we need them?"

"You should be fine. Just walk back-to-back and carry a long pointy stick. Also, keep an eye out for drop bears."

"Ha, there's no such thing, is there?"

"Technically no, we just call them bears because they're big and furry. They're actually spiders."

Traveller's tip: If you're an American visiting Australia and someone asks if you're American, the correct response is, "No, I'm Canadian." Though it may be shocking to learn, not everybody thinks Americans are quite as awesome as you know you are. I'm sure there are countries where the inhabitants will pretend to like you, like Mexico and Egypt, but Australians aren't great at pretending. Nobody in Australia gives a fuck that you're from Boston or that you patted a koala. If you can't bring yourself to pretend you're Canadian for five minutes, then at least try to tone down the whole 'guest on *Dr Phil*' thing.

You're probably shaking your head at this point because *you*, personally, are nothing like the guests on *Dr Phil*, but you are. You all are. I don't personally have anything against Americans, I married one, but the fact remains that all Americans can be summed up by three television shows: *Dr Phil*, *The Invicta Watch Hour on QVC*, and *Lip Sync Battle*.

I lasted less than a minute in the bog. The spiders weren't huge, averaging only an inch or two, but they made up for their size in volume. Hundreds ran up me; they ran into my ears, my nose, my eyes, and, when I screamed, my mouth. I stumbled as I fled in horror, becoming submerged to my chest, and when I stood I was wearing a writhing grey blanket. The next few minutes were a blur of climbing out of the bog, rolling on the ground while removing my clothing, and Mr Anderson beating me with his jacket as if I were on fire. I caught the bus home that evening.

The Andersons paid for my ticket and gave me fifty dollars; I knew it was pity money but took it anyway. I saw it more as compensation for having spiders in my mouth than payment for work completed. Also, when Mr Anderson beat me with his jacket, the metal zipper slider chipped one of my front teeth.

For the next few years, whenever I said the letter F, I whistled. It wasn't just a whistly noise, it was like blowing an actual whistle. It must have been the right shaped hole or something. I couldn't play a tune with it, it was just the one note, so it wasn't like a new skill. I never got the tooth fixed, I just learned to say 'th' instead of 'f' as it was better to have people think I had a lisp than to whistle, then one day I *tried* to whistle and couldn't, so I guess it sorted itself out.

I bought a pair of Adidas Romes with the money. They were surprisingly uncomfortable and squeaked a lot. For the first few weeks back at school, I squeaked and whistled everywhere I went like a sad one-man band. Additionally, I had abnormally large feet for my age and the white sneakers drew attention to them. Peter Jackson said I looked like I was wearing gigantic peeled bananas on my feet and everyone called me Banana Boy for several months until the school instigated a dress-code and everyone had to wear black shoes from Clarks.

Also, the cranberries weren't very good. They were too small, hard, and bitter for commercial use. The Andersons attempted to grow a second crop next season, but were forced to stop after they were caught illegally pumping water from the river.

I'm not entirely sure how the system works but apparently there's a regulated amount of water that you're allowed to take from the river, and flooding the cranberry bog had exceeded it by several million gallons. It made the front page of the local newspaper so I guess water theft is taken pretty seriously in Berri. I've no idea what the penalty was but the Andersons sold their property and moved to Adelaide a short time later. I think Mr Anderson sold kitchen cabinets. Mrs Anderson and my father had an affair about a year after that and Mr Anderson hanged himself in a motel bathroom. It was a whole thing at the time; my father stayed in a tent in our backyard for two weeks and my mother threw potatoes at Mrs Anderson in a supermarket parking lot and hit a baby in a stroller with one.

It was the third or fourth time my father had stayed in the tent, but the seventh or eighth time he'd had an affair. The first time he had an affair - or at least the first time he got caught - he stayed in a motel for several weeks. There was talk of divorce but then my parents went to marriage counselling and worked through it. He moved out again after the second, third, and fourth affairs, but the cost of hotel rooms added up so by the fifth affair, it made economic sense to pitch a tent in the backyard.

It was just routine by then anyway, a scripted performance. I'm not sure who for. Usually my father only stayed in the tent for three or four nights, the duration depended how long it took him to convince my mother she was to blame for letting herself go, and how attractive the woman my father slept with was.

Mrs Anderson was very attractive, she wore jean-shorts and was fit and tanned from working on the farm. Also, a week before my mother learned about the affair, my father had convinced my mother to get her hair coloured and cut into a bob exactly like Mrs Anderson's.

At the time, I didn't understand what the issue with the haircut was. I mean, technically, if my father was attracted to Mrs Anderson and wanted my mother to look more like her, it meant he was at least he was trying to make the marriage work. Maybe he should have asked before cutting the legs off a pair of her jeans, but his intentions were good. Really they should have tried to meet in the middle - like my father agrees to cut back on the affairs if my mother orders a bunch of different wigs.

"Yes, we could try marriage counselling again, that's certainly an option, or, and hear me out, we could spend that money on wigs instead."

"Wigs?"

"Yes, a bunch of them."

"What kind of wigs?"

"All the kinds. Coloured ones, curly ones, maybe a long blonde crimply one like Darryl Hannah's hair in *Splash*."

"Darryl Hannah?"

"I'm just using her as an example. Lots of people have long blonde crimply hair. Your sister for example."

I used the movie *Splash* in the dialogue above because my father took my sister and I to see it at the cinema four times. He only ever took us to two movies, *Splash* and *Urban Cowboy*, so that's a 4:1 ratio. I also saw *Splash* a few times when it was released on VHS, and several times since on television, so I feel somewhat qualified to state that at the end of the movie, when Darryl Hannah and Tom Hanks run to the edge of a pier and Darryl dives into the water, it's one of the worst dives ever captured on film. It's in the trailer if you want to check for yourself, but honestly, it's more of a belly-flop than a dive. You'd think a mermaid would know how to dive properly.

I have two theories about why the director didn't say, "Okay, cut, that was the worst dive I've ever seen and you'll have to do it again." The first is that it was a stunt person wearing the only wig and when he or she entered the water, the wig came off and was lost. The second is that the stunt person died from the dive.

Three hours and twelve minutes after we entered the tunnel, cars started moving again. I waited for a bit to make sure we wouldn't have to stop next to the Chick-fil-A bag, but whatever had caused the jam was fixed. We learned a short time later, once we had phone reception, there had been a minor rear-end crash which escalated into major road rage. Four people had been shot and killed, including a three-year-old girl, which kind of made us feel bad about all the complaining we'd done.

Someone's always having a worse day than you are. Probably in Philadelphia.

"You have to take the next right if you're going to take I76 to I81, it's an hour longer but there's no tolls. I'd get in the lane now if I were you."
"I'm not going that way, Tom. I've already told you that five times. I'm staying straight."
"There's tolls that way."
"I don't give a fuck. I'd pay a thousand dollars in tolls not to spend an extra hour in this car."
"It was propellors."

"What?"

"My *I Spy* clue, the P was for propellors."

"The ones on the ceiling?"

"Yes."

"You already did F for fans. This is why nobody wanted to play the game."

"Or you're just not very good at it. I'd get over now if you're going to take 176 to 181, it's an hour longer but there's no tolls."

It Will Be Okay

A photocopier service technician died in our agency last week. The name on his shirt said Rodney, I don't know what his last name was.

Rodney wasn't our regular photocopier service technician but he'd been in our office three or four times before; I think Xerox just sends out whoever is available at the time. Once they sent a young woman and my coworker Ben suddenly became interested in roller replacement and cartridge disposal logistics. He even asked if she'd like a coffee. Nobody offered Rodney a coffee. Nobody paid him much attention at all as he laid his tool bag down and grunted while kneeling to open a side panel on the copier.

Rodney was mid-fifties, overweight, and his light-grey collared shirt had yellow pit stains. I did notice that his face was shiny, but it was a passing observation.

"How's it going?" I asked as I walked past.
"Good," he replied.

It was automatic pleasantry; I may not have said anything if he hadn't glanced my way. It was the third time in as many weeks that the copier had broken and sometimes people, like objects, become white noise. I made myself a coffee and passed the copier again as I returned to my office.

"It's your main drive assembly."

"It is?"

"Yes it needs to be replaced. Common problem with the C750 model. They have plastic gear spindles and only last around 20,000 copies. Has it been jamming a lot?"

"Yes, all the time."

"New drive assembly should fix that... uh..."

"Are you okay? You're very sweaty."

"Yes, I'm fine... I just need to... uh... sit down for a moment."

"Can I get you a glass of water?"

"No, I... uh..."

Rodney lowered himself to the ground and sat with his back against the wall. He looked puzzled for a moment, then frightened. He made the "uh" noise a couple more times, slid sideways onto the carpet, and, through clenched teeth, said what sounded like the n-word but was probably just, "Nuuugahhhhhh!" I yelled for Melissa, our office manager, to call an ambulance.

"What for?"

"For Rodney, I think he's having a heart attack."

"Who's Rodney?"

"The photocopier guy!"

"How was I meant to know his name is Rodney?"

"Just call a fucking ambulance, Melissa!"

"Okay. Rude."

I knelt beside Rodney, placed a hand on his shoulder, and told him, "It will be okay." I hope it sounded sincere and comforting and not like a panicked plea. My yelling had brought Rebecca, our production manager, and Ben out of their offices; we exchanged wide-eyed stares that expressed, "What the fuck are we supposed to do?"

"Does anyone know CPR?" Rebecca asked.

Ben and I shook our heads. I did consider taking a CPR class many years ago when the company I worked for, Amcor, informed us that anyone taking the class received a pay bonus. After enquiring further, however, I learned the bonus was $17.00 and the class was held, outside of normal working hours, on a Saturday morning. I wasn't going to get up early on my day off for seventeen dollars. Also, one of the people who did do the course choked on a sandwich and died. It wasn't during the course, it was a few weeks later, so I'm not sure what the connection or point of adding that was. Maybe that the company should also have offered Heimlich manoeuvre classes with better financial incentives?

Melissa ran up the steps to inform us an ambulance was on its way. Ben knelt beside me. Rodney's face was contorted into the same expression weightlifters make when they're going for a world record; the muscles in his neck were taught and rivulets of sweat pooled in the folds. It was as if he was about to pop... then he relaxed and exhaled as if he'd been holding his breath. It sounded like a bicycle tire being let down.

Most of the staff were packed into the corridor by that point, mumbling about how they had thought about learning CPR but hadn't, and that they think the procedure is three quick pumps to the chest but it's probably best to leave it to the paramedics who should be arriving any moment.

Walter suggested splashing a bucket of water in Rodney's face, perhaps because he'd seen it in a movie. Jodie, our senior designer, stood with her hands on her cheeks and her mouth wide open like the kid in the movie *Home Alone*. The kid may also have done it in *Home Alone 2*, I'm not sure. It's been a while since I saw the movies. I remember there was a lady that fed pigeons in one of them, I think she was homeless. Gary, our account manager, asked, "Did he fix the photocopier?"

The paramedics arrived within a few minutes. I thought they'd yell "Clear!" and use those zappy things, but they just strapped Rodney to a stretcher and got him into the ambulance as quickly as possible. The entire process took less than two minutes and, if I'm being honest, was a bit of an anti-climax. I asked if Rodney was going to be okay and one of the paramedics said, "We'll do everything we can for him," which is probably the handbook response. Melissa rang the copier service company to let them know what had happened and the name of the hospital Rodney had been taken to. Two police officers arrived an hour or so later to take statements. We learned Rodney had been pronounced dead on his way to the hospital, so *technically* he hadn't died at the agency. Our art director, Mike, who had been out of the office at a 'client meeting' the whole time, walked in just as the police officers were leaving.

"Why were the police here?" he asked, "Did Melissa throw another can of soup at a bus?"

I put the apostrophes around 'client meeting' because it's a rule that if Mike is out of the office, he's in a client meeting. He doesn't tell anyone where he's really going because he once told Melissa he was going to the hairdresser and Melissa told a client that he was at the hairdresser. It was apparently the worst thing that had ever happened to him and several stern emails were written. Now, whenever a client calls for Mike and he's out, Melissa has to say, "I'm sorry, Mike is in a meeting with the CEO of Unilever." It's written on a post-it note stuck to the reception desk because she once forgot the Uni part of Unilever part and said, "I'm sorry, Mike is in a meeting with the CEO of levers."

"How fucking hard is it to remember Unilever? It's one of the largest brands on the planet."
"Not everyone cares about pens."
"What?"
"Unilever make pens."
"No they don't."
"I'm using one."
"That's a fucking Uniball."
"Oh, I might have been saying Uniball then because I don't look at the post-it note, I look at my pen."
"Are you serious?"
"Maybe you just shouldn't tell lies."

Once, when Melissa was in a bad mood, a client called for Mike and I overheard her say, "No, Mike's not here, he's in a pen meeting or something."

Melissa is generally in a bad mood but some days are worse than others. She knows she gets paid the least, so her mood is usually darkest on payday; she spends the day with her eyes narrowed and asks things like, "Is that a new jacket?"

If you confirm that it is indeed a new jacket, or pants, or shoes, she responds with, "Must be nice." I usually plan my attire accordingly.

"Is that a new suit?"
"Yes it is, thanks for noticing. It's Georgio Armani. I also bought a Tom Ford suit, in charcoal, but decided to wear grey today as it goes better with a white shirt."
"Must be nice. Is the shirt new as well?"
"This? No, I've had it at least a week. The shoes are new though."

I don't actually own a Tom Ford suit, I have no idea who Tom Ford even is, I just look up expensive brand names online to throw at Melissa because I know she knows them. Sometimes I get the brand names wrong on purpose as this seems to exasperate her more.

"Birdberry? Do you mean Burberry?"
"Yes, that might be it actually. I just liked the fabric. It's a yak and koala fur blend."

Someone named Beth called the agency the day after Rodney died. I was eating a sandwich in the boardroom and overheard Melissa on the phone. She was conveying the standard stuff about being 'sorry for your loss' and how 'it must be a difficult time', then stated, "I don't know, I wasn't with him, but I can ask David."

Apparently Beth wanted to know if Rodney had said anything before he died. I wasn't going to inform her he said, "Nuuugahhhhhh!" so I told Melissa to say his last words were, "Tell Beth I love her."

Really, there's no point trying to do something nice for anyone. How was I meant to know that Rodney's wife is named June and Beth is her sister? Perhaps get more information over the phone before involving me.

People really only use the 'tell my wife I love her' line in movies. The last thing my grandfather said was, "Pork chops for dinner," and he died comfortably in a hospital bed.

I Googled the most common thing people say before they die, and apparently it's, "Am I going to die?" I hope that just before I die, I have the mental capacity and opportunity to say something like, "Tell Seb there's 700K in cash hidden in the"

You'd have to know that the next thing you say is going to be the last thing you say though. If you managed to come up with something cool like, "In a world full of choices, choose kindness," then didn't die right away, you'd have to shut up and wait awkwardly. Probably looking around at everyone nodding. Nobody wants their last words to be, "No, hang on, I thought of a better one."

Watching someone die triggers contemplation of your own mortality. It's automatic, you don't get to decide that it's not a convenient time for such things because you have two logos and a 24-page annual report to be completed by Friday.

Rodney wasn't that much older than me and I chain-smoke. I'm actually astonished I don't already have cancer - I guess it's only a matter of time. There's not going to be any shocked expressions in the doctor's office.

"You have cancer, Mr Thorne."
"Oh my lord, how could this possibly happen?"
"You smoked a pack of cigarettes every day for 40 years."
"Yes, but I drink a lot of water."
"That doesn't have anything to do with it. Besides, a glass of water every four or five days isn't a lot."
"I also take multi-vitamins, the chewy ones. And I did yoga once."

This could be my last book. One of them is going to be. If this is my last, it's a little disappointing that more effort wasn't put it into it. I probably should have started writing it earlier but I say that every time and then other stuff gets in the way. Even if I had started writing this book earlier, I doubt it would include anything of real substance; anything life-changing for the reader. I guess you need to have a clear message to write a good book and I don't really have any message apart from *it will be okay*.

That's what I'd like Holly and Seb to know when I die; that it will be okay. It always is. I mean, I don't want it to be okay instantly, I'd like them to be a bit fucked up about it for a while. Six months seems like a reasonable timeframe before Holly starts dating again. Eventually I'd like her to meet someone, but not someone better looking and funnier than me. I want her to be happy, but not *too* happy. No upgrades. If he is better looking and funnier, then he should have a lisp. Also, I don't want him using my stuff. That includes the ATVs and my Global knife set. I should probably put all that in a will.

I know Seb will be okay. He's not overly bright or good looking, but he's tall. That counts for a lot. He'll need to learn at least one employable skill before he turns forty though. Nobody's going to pay to watch a middle-aged man stream *Minecraft* from a box under a bridge.

I'm not afraid of dying, or more so not afraid of being dead. Fearing the bit between being alive and being dead makes sense, otherwise there'd be no reason to avoid swimming at night or playing with snakes. It's more a fear of pain than of dying, the being dead part is someone else's problem. I don't believe in any of the gods so I'm not going to burn in flames, have to learn the harp, or come back as a moth.

I much prefer the whole 'stardust' thing. Momentary sparks of life. It makes more sense than sky wizards and doesn't require a book of instructions. You just kind of wing it, working out right from wrong along the way, while hopefully not fucking up everything too badly. Occasionally you interact with other momentary sparks of life and buy stuff.

It would be nice to be able to say, before I die, that I have no regrets. I have about a hundred though. Only a couple of those are significant however, the rest are minor regrets, like not buying Bitcoin when it was 12 cents and writing a love letter to my 5th grade teacher that included the sentence, "Nobody will ever love you like I do, other boys only like girls that have nice hair."

Sometimes I'll be lying in bed, about to fall asleep, and remember additional contents of that letter such as, "I'm the fastest runner out of Michael, Bradley, and me," and become flustered and have to get out of bed to Google obituaries.

It's sociopathic for anyone to have zero regrets in life, everyone has hurt someone and made poor decisions at some point. Lack of remorse pretty much defines antisocial personality disorder, it's on the test. Without remorse, there's no reparation, and reparation, either directly or indirectly, is the only thing that balances shitty actions out. Say, for example, you inadvertently set fire to a frog. Remorse itself doesn't create balance, you have to consciously commit to ensuring it never happens again and be extra kind to frogs from that moment on - maybe order them some live mealworms. There's no ratio to the rule, it's not ten happy frogs per one incinerated one, you have to be extra kind to frogs *for the rest of your life*.

And yes, there's a background story to the frog scenario but it's painful to recount. I'll just say that if you ever decide to kill a batch of weeds by splashing petrol on them and throwing a lit match, maybe poke among the weeds with a stick first. Nobody should have to witness a frog on fire, it's a lot more traumatic than you'd think. I had no idea frogs can scream. We have a koi pond in our backyard now, it's home to approximately fifty fat and happy frogs. They go through ten tubs of live mealworms each month, but I claim it as a business expense on my taxes because I can see the pond from my home office window. If I'm ever audited, I'm probably going to jail.

"And the $432.30 for squirrel mix, Mr Thorne?"
"There's also a tree outside my office window. It has a squirrel feeder in it shaped like a barn."

Reparation doesn't only apply to frogs of course. It probably wasn't the best example now that I think about it, but I'm not going to go back and rewrite an entire paragraph. Life's too short. Let's just say it's an analogy for poorly handled breakups or something. I did once break up with someone by fax. I saw her at a farmer's market a few years later and she threw a punnet of strawberries at me. I may have owed her money.

Actually, thinking back, I can't recall any of my previous relationships ending amicably. I'm not sure I'm even capable of such a thing. Maybe regrets are more about how you reacted to certain events, than the events themselves, and that's why certain people don't have them. People who grow herbs and own ducks most likely.

I've heard people state, after ending a relationship, stuff like, "We're still friends," and, "We both agreed it was best," but all my relationships have ended in resentment and tears. Usually mine; I was once shot in the leg with a speargun. I thought I still had the scar but looked for it just now and couldn't find it. Maybe the multi-vitamins fixed it.

I did find a grey leg hair though. I have a few grey hairs on my head but I hadn't thought about my leg hairs turning grey. If they all turn grey, my legs will look whiter than they are and I won't be able to wear shorts. I already have to shave my face daily because I have too many grey beard hairs. I'm not growing a Kenny Rogers beard.

Rodney was clean shaven the day he died. He'd shaved to about an inch below his neck line, leaving a sharp ridge of white chest hair that peaked out from his collared grey shirt. I checked my chest for grey hairs in the bathroom mirror this morning and discovered a four-inch one coming out of my left shoulder. I didn't even need tweezers to remove it, I just twirled it around a finger and yanked. I also noticed a wrinkle on my upper lip that I'm positive wasn't there last week.

I should probably get Botox and a box of Just for Men. Maybe do a plank.

Planks

Colorado is shaped like a rectangle. I mentioned this to Holly and she said, "And?" so I guess Americans are fine with this kind of thing. It must be difficult for Colorado's tourism department to work a rectangle into their marketing material though. Nobody's buying a Colorado shaped fridge magnet.

Right, I just Googled 'Colorado tourism' and they didn't even bother attempting to incorporate the shape of the state into their marketing material; they used a tree and mountain with the letter C instead. Must have been a gruelling two-minute logo development meeting for the creative agency that came up with it. It was probably a Friday afternoon and warm and someone had to leave early to pick up their kid from daycare.

With fifty states, I guess it's not surprising that America ended up with some rectangular ones. If you overlay a map of Australia onto a map of the United States, maybe on a light-box, the countries are basically the same size, but Australia only has six states. It makes it a lot easier to remember them all and none of them ended up rectangles.

America should consider reorganising its states to clean up the mess a bit. There's no need to have both a North Dakota and South Dakota for example; nobody wants to visit either. Apparently North Dakota's most famous tourism attraction is a meatpacking factory. How is that a thing? Just delete most of the states and remap the area into six or seven representative shapes that work well as fridge magnets. The middle states could be shaped like crosses and Wrangler jeans, the western states like popper bottles and Frenchies, and the upper eastern states like smug superiority. That last one might be a little difficult to represent visually but one of those prize ribbons they give the best pig at fairs might work. Florida can stay as it is because it's already flaccid penis shaped.

"Oh my God, David, you can't do that. We'd have to change the number of stars on our flag."

"Who cares? Your flag looks like it was designed by a six-year-old after eating a bag of sugar. Also, your country doesn't have a name."

"What are you talking about? We're the United States of America."

"Exactly. It's not a name, like Canada or Norway, it's a sentence. America is a continent, you're just a bit of it, and you've called yourself These Bits of America. It's like colonizing a bit of Asia and instead of coming up with a name for your bit of Asia, you call it These Bits of Asia."

"No, we'd be the United States of Asia."

"Other countries in Asia also have states. And names. You just have to be different, don't you?"

"We invented the shoe."

Holly made me fly to Colorado recently. Not 'made me' as in the human trafficking kind of made me, more of the acting disappointed that I wasn't as excited as her about it.

"Who's ready to spend 36 hours in airports? Woo!"

"36 hours?"

Yes, we have twelve stop-overs. I saved $38. Also, you're seated next to someone's support lizard on the first flight. Are you as excited as I am?"

"Yes."

"Don't lie. You haven't even packed yet. I've been packed since 1987. I just wish you were as excited about travelling as I am. I don't even want to go now. I wish I was dead."

If I *am* ever the victim of human trafficking and am being flown somewhere, I'll send an SOS to the flight assistant by blinking in Morse code. Here's a handy illustration showing the sequence should you ever need it:

Really, that illustration should show the eye opening between blinks. It won't work if you just sit there with one eye closed the whole time. That would just be a long dash. I don't know any Morse code apart from SOS so I'm not sure what a long dash means. It could mean 'Everything's fine' for all I know, which wouldn't be very helpful.

Okay, I just checked a Morse code chart and apparently one long dash is a T. Also, three blinks would just be an S so I'm not sure why I thought it was SOS. I remember reading something about firing a rifle three times into the air if you're lost in a forest, so maybe that was it. Also, I've heard of people tapping Morse code on walls but I have no idea how you manage a long tap. If I'm ever the victim of human trafficking, I'll probably just have to accept it and hope my new owners treat me well. I'd also like my own room.

The purpose of the Colorado trip was to check off one of Holly's 'bucket list' items: Doing yoga at the Red Rocks Amphitheatre. At least, she claimed it was on her bucket list. I haven't seen a written version. I doubt there's an actual list as she's just not that organized. We've had a magnetic 'shopping list' notepad on our refrigerator since 2017 and it's only ever had the single word 'carrots' written on it.

"Holly, can we throw out this refrigerator notepad? It just has the word carrots written on it and a squiggle from someone testing a pen."

"Why would we throw out a perfectly good notepad?"

"To reduce clutter and inconvenience. Every time I open the fridge door, things fly off and I have to pick them up. Can we at least get rid of some of these fridge magnets? There's about three hundred which adds a lot of weight. It's like opening the door of a bank vault."

"We're not throwing out any fridge magnets. Visitors won't know where we've been."

We have so many fridge magnets, birds regularly crash into our kitchen window. Half of the magnets aren't even from places we've visited; they're places Holly's brother and stepsister visited and brought back for us. I don't give a fuck that they toured the M&M factory in Tennessee. We also had a colourful plastic alphabet on our fridge for a few days but Seb kept writing 'Dad is gay' so I threw them out. I did initially attempt to alter it to '*Seb* is gay' but I dropped the letter S and it went under the fridge. Whatever goes under the fridge belongs to the fridge.

I don't really have a bucket list. I have no desire to jump out of a plane, swim with sharks, or visit Greece. There are way too many Greek people in Greece. You know what they're like; always fixing nets on beaches and eating yoghurt. We had a Greek neighbour when I lived in Australia and he once threw a peach at me. I would like to own a lot of bamboo one day, so maybe that counts as a bucket list item. I'm a big fan of bamboo.

I'm not a big fan of travelling and I'm even less of a fan of yoga. Yoga isn't just about bending and balancing; they make you do planks. Lots of planks. Planks aren't even the worst part about yoga - it's the people who do yoga. They pretend to like quinoa and act as if they've received some kind of deep message from the Universe by standing on one leg and rubbing a metal bowl with a stick. Sadly, the message didn't include the phrase, "Remember, the only person who thinks the rubbing bowl noise is pleasant is the one making it."

We actually have about thirty rubbing bowls* in our house. Holly kept ordering them from Amazon until she found one she liked the tone of. I use one for cereal, others are distributed throughout the house to collect things in - dust and dead moths mainly. Holly also ordered a tiny metal squashed-orange-shaped thing called a tongue

---

* Apparently the correct term is Singing Bowl. It's only singing if you'd describe the sound a dog-sized mosquito would make as singing though. Really, it's more of a whine with scratching accompanied by, "Okay, I've got it... no, hang on... wait... okay, that's it. Nice, isn't it? No wait..."

drum. You play notes by hitting it with what looks like a toothpick with a bead on the end. Apparently it looked bigger on Amazon. It came with an instructional booklet on how to play *Mary Had a Little Lamb*, but Holly prefers to compose her own masterpieces.

"Play the *Bong Bing Bong Bong* tune again, Holly. I find it relaxing. Especially while I'm watching television."
"Is that sarcasm? Right, well I don't want it to play it anymore. Thanks for ruining my dream of becoming the best tongue drum player in the world. It was number 136 on my bucket list. I wish I was dead."
"Just skip to 137; owning a fruit stand on a beach."
"That's not 137, 137 is riding an ostrich."

It could be worse of course. I once shared an apartment with a guy who owned an ocarina. It sounded like pigeons fighting.

It's easy to criticise though, I don't know how to play any musical instruments apart from the triangle. I've never actually played a triangle but it doesn't look that difficult. I mean, it doesn't even have a name. Its name is its shape. I attended an orchestral performance of Vivaldi's *Four Seasons* a few years back and I couldn't help but wonder the whole time if the triangle player got paid as much as the oboe and flugelhorn players. You don't really hear about famous triangle players. Or perhaps I'm just not familiar with any because I'm not in the loop. They could be the most highly respected members of an orchestra for all I know.

"I met someone."

"You did? What's his name?"

"Timothy."

"What does he do?"

"He's a triangle player with the New York Philharmonic."

"Oh, that's... wait, you don't mean Timothy Roberts, do you? I wept at his clear-toned yet shimmering timbre in Mahler's *Fifth Symphony*."

"Yes, that's him. He's very talented."

"You have to introduce me. I have all his CDs."

I did take piano lessons when I was ten. My teacher's name was Mrs Williams and I was dropped off at her flat Thursday evenings for an hour. My mother got her number from the window of our local butcher. For the first half of each lesson, Mrs Williams yelled at me for not practicing. For the second half, she told me stories about every cat she'd ever owned.

"And here's a photo of Matilda. She died in 1943. She was such a scamp. She'd hide behind a door and attack my leg as I entered the room. I went through a lot of pantyhose back then and pantyhose weren't easy to come by because of the war. The government needed the nylon to make parachutes out of."

I had no idea what I was meant to be learning. Mrs Williams said I was the worst student she'd ever had. Sometimes she called me Dennis and make me fix stuff around her apartment. Once, she made me run a bath and help her in. I didn't tell my parents as that might have meant going to a different teacher and having to learn the piano.

Mrs Williams didn't answer the door one evening. Apparently she slipped on an ice cube and struck her head as she fell. My mother made me attend her funeral and, during the service, the speaker at the podium indicated towards a piano and asked, "Would one of Mrs William's students like to play something they learned for us?"

There was only one other kid at the service and he was in one of those motorized wheelchairs that you control with a stick in your mouth.

"Go up there, David."
"What? No."
"Go up there and play the piano right now."
"I can't. I'm too sad about Mrs Williams being dead."

My mother grabbed and squeezed my arm - roughly like she had a robot hand - stood me up, and declared, "David wants to play the piano for us. Don't you, David?"

I'd hoped that at some point between leaving my seat and arriving at the piano, I'd come up with a viable excuse not to play. I hadn't though, even though I walked in slow-motion.

I could have stated, "Sorry, I can't play because my mother squeezed my arm really hard like a robot and now I can't move my fingers," but that would have meant serious recriminations the moment she had me out the door. I would have needed to add something about it not being the first time she'd abused me and that I was scared to leave with her. Carter, the foster kid, had his own television in his bedroom and a poster of a cylon above his bed. He didn't even have to call his foster parents mum and dad; he called them Geoff and Stacey.

"What do you want me to play?" I asked. I have no idea why as I was in no position to take requests.
"Whatever you like," the speaker replied, "Something Mrs Williams taught you."

I nodded and stared at the keys. My head felt like it was made of burning prickles. "Okay, how hard can playing the piano be?" I asked myself. I poked a couple of keys randomly and it didn't sound too bad. I poked a few more and there was kind of a tune. I repeated the tune to make it appear intentional and was pretty pleased with the result.

"Oh my god," I thought, "I'm actually good at the piano."

Swept away with my newly discovered talent, I started exploring the entire keyboard and furiously tapping the foot pedals. At one point I used an elbow. To my ears, it was pretty much the greatest piano composition ever performed; I'd receive a standing ovation when I finished and people would cry and tell me I have a gift.

It's probably how Holly feels when she's playing her rubbing bowls and tongue drum.

I was yanked backwards off the piano chair by my collar. "I'm so sorry," my mother said to the people seated as she dragged me down the aisle and out the door, "we don't know what's wrong with him."

I blame lack of encouragement for not becoming a famous pianist. When Seb was 10, I bought him a trumpet. I'm rather sensitive to loud noises so he had to keep it at his mother's house.

Really, my lack of musical talent probably just comes down to laziness. Learning to play an instrument is like learning another language and I can't even be bothered with English half the time. I know most of the commonly used English words, like envelope and rubber, but up until fairly recently I thought the word nonplussed was a math term, and cajole was a type of stew with clams. I still have no idea what a lychee is.

It's entirely possible laziness is also the reason I don't have a bucket list. Or maybe complacency is a better word. A lot of bucket list-based activities involve leaving the house and all my furniture is there and set up how I like it.

"Nothing grows in the comfort zone."
"Bamboo does. It grows in all zones. Besides, I just bought new pillows."
"That's money you could have spent on spelunking or a fried scorpion on a stick."

I doubt I'd travel at all if it wasn't for Holly. I'd probably spend the money on plants instead. Still, having travelled more in the last ten years than I ever did before we met, I have grown to dislike the process slightly less than I used to. Maybe the real reason I've never cared much for exploring new places was not having someone to explore them with.

Or maybe it's a resignation thing, like taking a child to the beach; there's a lot of stuff to carry and you've got better things to do, but it's school break and you have do something with them otherwise you'll look like a bad parent. You get a bit of sun though and the beach wasn't as crowded as you feared it might be.

Colorado is nice enough. It has mountains and trees. Someone who has lived their entire life on the Nullabor Plain might be more impressed but I don't have too many complaints apart from the state being rectangular and having to fly into Denver.

I'm sure Denver has some nice areas, areas where homeless people don't throw bottles of urine at you when you refuse to buy a bag of used Brillo pads, but I didn't see any. Denver's entire economy is based on stolen catalytic converters. Its tourism slogan is, *There's only a 4% chance you'll be stabbed.*

Our flight landed in Denver late-afternoon. Originally Holly and I had planned to see downtown and eat, but drove out of Denver an hour later. It would have been sooner but there was a bit of traffic. People follow the boating rule of driving in Denver - larger vessels have right of way - and Avis assigned us a toaster on wheels called the Scion xD. For those unfamiliar with the Scion xD, it's a 4-cylinder design atrocity with around 20 horsepower. It takes twelve minutes to get to sixty, unless you're on a slight incline, in which case it doesn't get to sixty. Ours was bright orange. Voices were raised and opinions given, but Avis doesn't give a fuck.

"You booked a small SUV 'or similar', sir."
"How is the Scion similar? SUV stands for sports utility vehicle and it's none of those things. Why can't we have that white Jeep?"
"Are you an Avis Preferred member, sir?"
"I'd prefer the Jeep."
"The Jeep is reserved for Avis Preferred members."
"Do you have anything else available?"
"I'll check... hmm... we do have a Nissan Cube."
"We'll just take the Scion."

Avis, and most of the other car rental agencies, sold a lot of their fleet during the pandemic to survive financially. Nobody wanted to rent cars during that time and now that people do, there's none to rent. You'd think the agencies could just buy more cars, but there aren't any due to a shortage of microchips caused by everyone buying big-screen televisions and variable-speed vibrators during the pandemic. It's a cause-and-effect thing, like not being able to afford benzoyl peroxide because you spent all your money on chocolate.

We had to catch a shuttle bus from the airport to Avis and I wondered at the time why everyone leapt off and sprinted towards the office the moment we arrived. It was like that scene in the movie *World War Z* where the fast zombies rush a wall, but with luggage. An old lady elbowed me in the neck and I'm pretty sure it was on purpose. Turns out it's first in, best choice, and those in the know had probably seen the Scion on the lot.

We drove through Columbine, a suburb of Denver, on the way to our hotel. Columbine is best known for a turning point in American history; on April 20, 1999, two students of Columbine High School shot and killed 12 students and one teacher. Twenty-one additional people were injured by gunshots. Within weeks, the American people, having agreed the safety of its children took priority over personal desires and political agendas, banned the sale of firearms nationwide. There have been no school shootings since.

Our hotel was satisfactory; it had a balcony, coffee machine, and a king-sized bed. It was also close to the Red Rocks Ampitheatre and a Mediterranean restaurant. Finding a decent Mediterranean restaurant when Holly and I travel is a priority, as there isn't one in the village we live in. People here don't want "weird Arab food", they want steak and macaroni & cheese and burgers with a big pickle on the side. The most popular restaurant in our village is called Cracker Barrel, which is also a brand of cheese. Holly's father, Tom, won't even eat mushrooms because they're too exotic. His idea of fancy international cuisine is Outback Steakhouse; it's posh because they bring you a wooden board with a loaf of black bread on it. He won't eat the bread, because bread is meant to be white and sliced, but he does like the bloomin' onions.

"Are you getting a bloomin' onion, David? I bet you miss bloomin' onions."

"Why would I miss them, Tom?"

"Because that's what you eat in Australia."

"Why do you say that every time we eat here? There's no bloomin' onions in Australia. It's an American construct and I'd never even heard of it before I moved here."

"Best thing to come out of Australia. I like the sauce. I'm getting a bloomin' onion and the Melbourne porterhouse. What are you getting, Maria?"

"I don't know, I'm not that hungry so I might just get an aussietizer. Maybe the kookaburra wings."

I ask for 'battered and fried mushrooms' when we eat at Outback Steakhouse because I refuse to call them Sydney shrooms. It's like opening an American themed restaurant in Australia with dishes called the mobility scooter burger and bald eagle wings.

"Welcome to the No Healthcare Steakhouse. Would you care to try the freedom dip?"

"What is it?"

"It's a neon-yellow block of cheese with candy corns poked into it. A very popular dish in America. They all eat it."

"No, I think I'll have the Guantánamo Bay guacamole."

"With or without Jim Crow jerky sprinkles?"

Outback Steakhouse's slogan is 'no rules' so technically you're allowed to take the cutlery. We have around twenty of their steak knives and three wooden bread boards. Also a big poster of an old stamp.

There are literally thousands of images of the Red Rocks Ampitheatre online, and it's been featured on hundreds of album covers, so describing it would be redundant. That may seem like lazy writing, and was, but, really, the name pretty much covers it; it's an ampitheatre surrounded by red rocks. There are also thousands of descriptions online if you need a better one. Most mention the awe-inspiring views and natural acoustics, very few mention the five-thousand steps you have to climb to get there. If they do, it'll be in paragraph eighteen after the bit about bringing a light jacket in case it rains. Really it should be the first thing mentioned. Maybe in bold.

"Have I mentioned my bathmophobia, Holly? It's the fear of steps or inclines. It's a real thing and I have it."

"No you don't, you're just lazy. Besides, 5000 steps is a wild exaggeration, there's only 386."

"That's a very specific number, meaning you knew about the steps and chose to hold the information from me."

"Yes, because I knew you'd complain."

"I'm not complaining. All I'm saying is that there has to be a hidden elevator somewhere for wheelchair access. Maybe disguised as a rock. Look for rectangular markings."

Excitement drove Holly up the steps, I used a blend of anger and refusal to show weakness in front of yoga people. For all their manta rays and shakira charts, yoga people can be very judgemental. If you're not wearing Prana or Athleta and have a bit of belly because you've been too busy to play tennis lately, they can be downright cruel with their thoughts. They may smile and nod but you can tell they're thinking, "I'm an elk on the reincarnation wheel and you're still a beetle."

I was wearing cargo shorts and a Jet Propulsion Laboratories t-shirt. I've also been pretty busy lately and tennis is the only sport I play because A. it isn't a team sport and B. there's a decent amount of distance and a net between you and the other player.

There were chairs halfway up the steps to the ampitheatre where you could take a break, but an old woman was having a stroke in one while three or four other old women fanned her with their yoga mats.

"Just take deep breaths, Iris."
"I'm feeling a little better. Give me a moment and I'll try to make it the rest of the way."
"No, it's okay, we'll turn back when you're ready."
"I don't want to disappoint anyone."
"It's fine, really, none of us knew about the steps."

I don't have step-climbing-calves. I assume the same kind of people that can run in soft sand can easily handle 386 steps, but my legs were done by the time we reached the top. It wasn't the 'give me a moment' kind of done either, it was the 'call in a rescue helicopter' kind. I wobbled after Holly like one of those marathon finishers who no longer remembers a life without pain or their own name. You know the ones, sometimes they have a trickle of poo running down a leg.

Due to my inability to match Holly's three steps at a time, the yoga session had already started by the time we found a space and laid out our yoga mats. I'd purchased my yoga mat from Target the night before; it cost $12.95 and had a picture of a whale on it. I would have preferred a plain yoga mat but they were six-dollars more. Holly brought her yoga mat from home, it's by Manduka and cost around $200 because it's made out of recycled pen lids or something. I think my mat was made out of cellophane.

"It's very thin."
"That makes it easier to roll up and carry."

Everyone was on their hands and knees so I copied them. It was basically the 'just get it over with' version of doggy style so little effort was required. We've all been there. On the stage below us, a girl in huge puffy pants with a microphone on her head said, "Okay, now step back to plank." Which is the moment I discovered there are planks in yoga.

None of the pictures I'd seen of people doing yoga showed planks. They showed ponytailed women silhouetted against a sunrise, balancing on one leg or sitting with their legs crossed. I figured I could manage the one leg pose and kind of do the cross-legged one; my body only bends two or three ways and they're slight bends at best. It functions adequately for general tasks, like sleeping, sitting, and driving, but it isn't the kind that planks. It takes stomach muscles to plank and the only exercise my stomach gets is being sucked in when Holly enters the bathroom while I'm in the shower.

"Um, the bathroom is occupied."

"I've seen it all before. I just need to brush my teeth."

"I'm pretty sure the door was locked."

"Yes, but there's a little hole in the knob that you can poke a pin into that unlocks it."

"There's a reason I lock it."

"I thought it was because you're scared a murderer might come in and stab you while you're in the shower. Are you sucking your stomach in?"

"No."

"It looks like you are."

That moment where you have your head under the water while washing out shampoo or conditioner would definitely be the worst time for a murderer to attack you. Wet, naked, and taken by surprise, you'd be in no position to defend yourself. You wouldn't even have time to suck in your stomach. Sometimes when Holly is showering, I sneak in, put my face near the glass, and loudly state, "Excuse me." She screams and goes wobbly, and cried once, so she knows how vulnerable you are in there. All I'm asking for is a little consideration.

Also, it might be a hereditary trait because once when I was home alone and taking a shower, Tom poked his head into the bathroom and said, "Just dropping off a pumpkin."

There are actually about thirty different kinds of planks in yoga. They call them different names, like Chatarunga and Phalakasana, to disguise the fact, but they're definitely planks. There's side planks and high planks and upward planks and extended planks, there's even advanced planks for those who find standard planks too easy. I couldn't even manage the standing on one leg pose and I've always thought I had good balance. I stood up on a paddleboard once.

There was a moment though, when the sun rose and turned the umber monoliths a vibrant orange, that almost made the planks worth it. And not every pose was a plank; the one at the end where you lay on your back and listen to a gong was okay. The gong was a bit annoying though.

"Did you have fun?" Holly asked.

"It met certain expectations. Exceeded others."

"I can tick that off my bucket list now."

"Yes, what's next? Burpees at the Grand Canyon?"

"Ooh, yoga at the Grand Canyon would be cool. I bet they have it there."

"Yes, we should base all our future vacations on yoga. We could do it in every state. We'll start a blog called *50 States of Yoga* that documents our journey and sell t-shirts with an outlined map of the USA that people can colour in with a sharpie as they tick states off. Once the money rolls in, we can quit our jobs and be full-time travelling yoga people."

"I'd love that."

"I bet you would. The only problem with the whole plan is that I'm never doing yoga again."

"What, never?"

"Never. You all pretend it's something spiritual and life-changing, but it's just planks. I'm adding yoga to my reverse bucket list."

"What's a reverse bucket list?"

"It's a growing list of things I don't want to do and places I don't want to visit. Yoga is just above eating at Outback Steakhouse with your parents."

Holly registered the name 50statesofyoga.com during our drive back to the airport. We're doing yoga at the Grand Canyon in a few weeks and staying in a transparent bubble pod.

The Royal Hotel

The worst hotel I've ever stayed in was The Royal Hotel in Orange, New South Wales. Don't be misled by the use of the word royal, there was no opulence, it's the type of place recently divorced men in their forties commit suicide in.

I worked for a small branding agency in Australia called de Masi jones at the time. I travelled occasionally for meetings but it was always begrudgingly; there were no white beaches or fancy restaurants, it was always the cheapest and closest hotel to the airport and service station sandwiches. The accommodations were arranged by our secretary, a bushpig named Shannon, and we didn't get along that well. I'm not sure what her problem with me was as I'm quite amiable. I gave her a three-pack of underarm deodorant for Secret Santa one year. We were only meant to spend a maximum of ten dollars and I'm pretty sure the three-pack was closer to twelve.

My room at The Royal didn't even have its own bathroom. I had to share a bathroom with everyone else on my floor and it looked like it hadn't been cleaned since the 70s.

Tiles were missing and those that weren't were brown and furry like a wet otter. You had to flush the toilet with a bucket of water and the shower drain was blocked with a wad of hair the size of a basketball. It was a tub shower and when the water rose to ankle height, the wad of hair floated around like seaweed in a current. When I stepped out, my feet looked like a hobbit's.

My room looked like a youth remand centre cell or a taxation department interview room. There were no pictures on the wall or welcome chocolates on the pillow, just a single bed, a wardrobe, and a box of empty pickle jars. The lock on my door was broken and the door jamb was splintered, it looked like it had been kicked in. When I rang the front desk to inform them about the lock and request a different room, I was told they were fully booked and to push my bed in front of the door if I was concerned about security. When I moved the bed, I discovered a prosthetic leg under it. Why would someone leave a prosthetic leg behind unless they died?

"Hello, it's David Thorne in room 17 again. I moved the bed like you told me and found a prosthetic leg under it."
"A leg?"
"Yes, a prosthetic one. It has a sock and shoe on it. What do you want me to do with it?"
"You can keep it if you like."

Around 2am, I was awakened by a loud knock on the door. It may actually have just been a normal volume knock, but the bed was against the door and my head was only a few inches away.

"Who is it?" I asked, startled and confused.
"It's Trevor."
"Who? What do you want?"
"Let me in."
"What? Why?"
"Just let me in. I've got something for you."
"What is it?"
"Just open the door."
"Do you work here? Is this about the leg?"
"What? It's Trevor."
"I was sleeping."
"Fine, I'll slip it under the door."

I heard something being shoved under the door and footsteps walking away. I waited, until I was sure the person had left, then turned on the light and reached under the bed to check what it was.

It was a folded A4 piece of paper with a drawing of a sword on it.

PMS Orange 021

Seb has been growing a beard and I'm not pleased about it. It's as if one moment he was a fresh-faced teenager, and the next, a filthy old peasant from the middle-ages. The kind that peers a lot and wears one of those leather hats.

"Ist thou a beggar or an alley-rapist?"
"Neither m'lord, simply a humble peasant making his way to the kitchen to microwave a Hot Pocket."
"Be thee on your journey then, I wish not to gaze upon such wretched facial hair a second longer."
"Tis the fashion m'lord."

It isn't a pleasant beard to look at; it doesn't conjure up images of cutting down trees or hiking the Appalachians, it's more of a 'singed koala after a forest fire' image. It's scraggly and wiry and astonishingly orange. There's no history of orange hair on my side of the family, or on Seb's mother's, so I should probably get a paternity test done. He already looks homeless so I won't have any qualms about throwing him out if he's not mine. He can keep his clothes and borrow a suitcase - I'll need it back because all of our suitcases are by Away and cost more than his car.

"Honestly, Seb, it's like staring at a homeless Scottish man's crotch. One with a lot of static."

"Don't look at it then. It just needs to grow in a bit. I think it looks good."

"Don't lie. There's no way you aren't disappointed with how it turned out. Nobody hopes for such a thing. I'll give you fifty dollars to shave it off."

"Really?"

"You'd shave it off for fifty dollars?"

"Yes."

"Well, you can't like it too much then. If you really liked it, you would have made a counteroffer; I would have gone up to a hundred. I retract my offer and will instead wait it out. Eventually you'll admit to yourself that the beard is a bit more orange and bird-nestish than you were expecting and shave it off. I give it three days, maybe a week if you don't have to leave the house for anything. I can be patient."

"When have you ever been patient?"

"Fine, you called my bluff, I'll give you a hundred dollars to shave it off right now."

I once had to pay Seb to cut his toenails. They clacked when he walked barefooted through the house like someone tapping pencils on a desk. I discovered one while vacuuming a few days later and thought it was a deer antler.

Sharp Knives

A week before I turned ten, my sister Leith told me I was getting a diving knife for my birthday; the type skindivers strap to their leg and use to fight off sharks or free dolphins from nets. I was pretty excited about it and didn't think to question why my parents would get me a diving knife. They hadn't, they gave me an alarm clock for my birthday. When I asked Leith why she told me I was getting a diving knife, she said, "I just thought it was funny."

What's funny about a diving knife? For about four years afterwards, whenever Leith and I argued, I'd end each altercation with, "And you still owe me a diving knife." Which didn't make any sense.

Carter's foster parents bought him a remote-controlled helicopter for his tenth birthday - not like the cheap ones you can get on Amazon nowadays, it had a petrol engine and the remote control had a neck strap. I asked Carter if I could fly it but I wasn't allowed to because replacement blades cost thirty dollars. Which was probably double what my parents spent on the alarm clock.

There was no volume control on the alarm clock and it only had one sound; an obnoxiously loud, high-pitched digital scream similar to a smoke alarm or forklift. The first time I set the alarm, my father burst into my bedroom looking terrified and yelling. We couldn't work out how to turn it off, and yanking the plug out of the wall didn't work as it had a backup battery, so he stomped on it until it went eeeeeeep. I'd had it for two days.

I'm not a big fan of alarms, I figure if you don't wake up naturally, you're not meant to wake up. It means I'm often late to work, or not there at all if I don't get up before 4pm. There's no point getting ready and driving there just to listen to people complaining for fifteen minutes about having to carry the workload for others. I'm pretty sure they're talking about Gary as he takes really long lunch breaks and poos at least five times per day.

Holly gets up at 6am so sets alarms for 5am, 5.10am, 5.20am, 5.30am, 5.40am... Each alarm has a different sound, including marimba drums, a delivery truck, and Harry Styles saying, "It's time to wake up my lovely." For the odd occasion when I do have to be at work on time, I have one alarm, of ducks quacking, and I set it for the time I need to get up. The quacking wakes me immediately as I think, 'Ducks? You can't sleep next to a pond, David, you'll roll over and fall in.'

I have a healthy fear of drowning - or more a fear of being trapped underwater. When I was twelve, a kid from school named Nathan invited me to his house to swim and tried to drown me.

Nathan and I weren't exactly friends, but we were paired in science class and hung out during recess and lunch a few times - mainly because neither of us had anyone else to hang out with. I'd had a falling out with my best friend Michael over skateboard wheels, or maybe the bearings, and Nathan didn't have any friends because he once wore a Care Bears t-shirt to school. It had been well over a year since the shirt incident but kids don't let that kind of thing go. I didn't witness the shirt personally, I must have been off school that day, but apparently you could tell from the cut and wide neck that it was a girl's shirt.

Nathan's parents were wealthy; I think his dad was an accountant. Their house was in a nicer neighbourhood than ours, a neighbourhood with hedges and a jogging park. Our neighbourhood had a sinkhole.

Technically it wasn't a real sinkhole, just a deep bog, but it had a fence around it with warning signs because a kid had drowned there. Apparently he jumped off the edge into deep water and his feet got stuck in the mud. Which couldn't have been a pleasant death. Michael and I climbed over the fence once but we didn't stay long because there was ghost story going around about the boy coming out of the water and dragging you in. There were also a lot of mosquitos.

My mother dropped me off a few houses down from Nathan's house because there was a shiny Mercedes in the driveway. We drove a Ford Fairmont with a coat hanger for an aerial.

"Just don't do anything to embarrass me."
"You? Like what?"
"All the things. Be polite and don't walk through the house with wet feet. And if Nathan's mother asks what type of carpet we have, tell her it's Berber."
"Why would she ask about our carpet?"
"You might forget not to walk through their house with wet feet and if Nathan's mother says, "Do you walk through your own house with wet feet?" you should say, 'No, because we have expensive Berber carpet.'"
"What?"
"Just try to be normal."

I've no idea why Berber carpet was a thing in the 80s and 90s. It felt like a Brillo pad and only came in five colours: blue, green, beige, light beige, and lighter beige. Ours was beige but the choice hadn't been easy. The Berber consultant had to come to our house three times to show my mother samples - the third time, he left them with her. The samples were all together, hinged like a giant wooly book, and my mother took it everywhere she went for two weeks. She said it was to get other people's opinion on the colours, but she'd already ordered the beige, so really it was just to let people know she was getting new carpet.

"Oh, you like the blue? Yes, it's lovely, all the colours are lovely, but I think the blue might date. Beige is timeless don't you think? You can't go wrong with beige."
"Sure. Is that all for you today, Maam? Just the milk and bread?"
"Yes, thank you. So you really prefer the blue over the beige?"

We only bought new carpet because our old carpet melted in a house fire. It's not as if we had carpet money to throw about at whim. Nobody who saw the book thought, "Oh my God, she's getting new carpet, she must be rich." They probably just thought we needed new carpet because ours was shit. Or didn't think anything because nobody gives a fuck about carpet. .

My mother even tried to get me to take the carpet book to school but I wasn't having it. There's no show & tell in high school and even if there were, I wouldn't show a book of carpet samples. She got worse once the carpet was installed; she vacuumed twice-daily, set up checkpoints for shoes, and said, "Where are you going with that?" whenever she saw anyone holding a drink or food. You could be standing outside and she'd say it.

Also, I should add that my father did his own oil changes, and, to dispose of the old motor oil, he poured it into the toilet and flushed it. I'm not sure what you're meant to do with old motor oil but I think it involves taking it somewhere so it can be disposed of in an ecologically sound manner. My father said it lubricated the pipes, so was actually good for the plumbing, but I assume he just couldn't be bothered dealing with it. The day he carried a bucket of used motor oil through the house and the handle broke, was the day he and my mother began their third trial separation.

The first two were because he fucked someone else.

The house fire, in case you were wondering, was caused by my sister hanging her dressing gown on a chair next to a space heater. This was before clothing had fire safety ratings and the dressing gown was probably made out of lint and wax.

 **Wow**

There's a sentence on page 114 about lint and wax that was copied verbatim from line 21, page 137, of his earlier book, Sixteen Different Flavours of Hell. It made me angry and if I could give this book ten-thousand minus stars I would.

I'd been to Nathan's house once before. It was for his tenth birthday party a couple of years earlier. It wasn't much of a party as there were only two other kids there and one of those was his older brother, Stevie, who had something wrong with him. I'm not sure what it was but he shook a lot and dribbled. Stevie opened one of Nathan's presents, I think it was a Lego X-wing fighter, and Nathan had a serious meltdown. There was a lot of screaming and throwing things and Nathan was sent to his room. Nathan's mother rang our parents to come and collect us early and we were forced to play musical chairs while we waited. We had to always let Stevie have a chair so I'm not sure what the point was. When I asked, I was told to wait outside on the front door step.

The pool was large and rectangular with a diving board and an electric pool cover. After jumping in and splashing about for a bit, Nathan suggested we have a contest to see who could dive in and swim the farthest underwater.

When it was my turn, Nathan activated the pool cover.

I had my eyes closed, due to the chlorine, but opened them when I heard a whirring sound and felt the sun disappear. I swam up and tried to lift the cover, but had no leverage as my feet didn't touch the bottom. I turned, tried to outswim the closing cover, but it was well past me by that time. It didn't occur to me to swim to the edge; my only chance I thought, was to swim to the shallow end. There was a moment when I *knew* I wasn't going to make it and yelled, swallowing water, but then my foot brushed the bottom. I stood, forcing the cover up with my head, but it was heavy and suction caused the water to rise with it. There was no air pocket.

It would have been the perfect time to have a diving knife strapped to my leg.

Holly actually gave me a knife for my birthday this year. It's not a diving knife though, it's an EDC pocket knife. EDC stands for Every Day Carry but I'm not the type of guy who carries a pocket knife everywhere they go. I realise carrying one might come in handy if you need to cut string or open an Amazon box, but I generally open boxes in our kitchen and there's an assortment of knives in there. I don't recall the last time I needed to cut string. Also, I don't wear the same pants every day and I don't have the mental discipline to remember to transfer a pocket knife to each day's pant selection.

People who always have a knife on them probably don't own a lot of pants; maybe a pair of Wranglers for daily-wear and another 'best' pair of Wranglers for dining at Olive Garden. I've seen photos of Holly's past boyfriends and they all look like two-pants guys. The type of guys who work in a warehouse, maybe driving a forklift. One of them looks like he's blind - you know that look blind people have. They always seem to have a straight fringe. Regardless, whenever Holly needed string cut or a box opened, the boyfriend probably said, "I got this, babe."

Women like that kind of thing. It's a built-in ancestral thing from when we lived in caves and knife-based duties were the guy's responsibility.

"Grok, there's a sabre-toothed tiger in the bathroom. I'd stab it myself but if I touch your knife, menstrual spirits will enter the blade and it will need to be thrown off a cliff."
"I got this, babe."

I pushed harder against the cover, with my head and hands, and a crease formed, allowing air to rush in from the edge. It was probably like when mothers find untapped reserves of strength and lift trees off babies. The cover immediately became lighter and I stood fully, coughing up water and gasping for air.

Then Nathan jumped onto the cover near me, forcing me back under; it felt like I'd been hit on the head by a king-sized mattress. His weight also pulled the cover from the edge and I swam for the gap - reaching the side and pulling myself out. I laid on the edge of the pool, sobbing, as Nathan clumsily attempted to crawl off the cover - laughing at how difficult it was.

There was a small shed by the pool where floaties and cleaning supplies were kept. Leaning against it was a long metal pole with a net on the end.

Nathan's mother, holding two cans of Coke, stepped through a sliding glass door at the exact moment I swung the pole in a wide arc and struck Nathan in the face. The blow sent him backwards onto the cover - a splash of blood from his nose seemed to hang in the air for a moment before hitting and mixing with the water that had pooled on top. It probably looked worse than it was; there'd been some air-resistance from the net.

The cans of Coke erupted in froth as they hit the ground and I remember thinking, "Why did she open them?"

I don't like people opening cans for me. It's like sticking your tongue out and having someone touch it with their thumb and finger.

I waited on the front door step for my mother to collect me. There'd been a lot of yelling and there was more when my mother arrived. Nathan's mother threatened to press charges even though the cover on the pool supported my version of events. She also suggested there was something wrong with me and I should be tested. Which was kind of rich coming from the mother of a child who had attempted to drown me. I assumed my mother would say something to that effect but instead she just nodded and said, "We did have him tested but they couldn't work out what's wrong with him."

I don't recall a specific event that warranted my parents taking me to a child psychologist; it may have been a series of events, or they just wanted to be able to say, "Sorry, he has x" for all future events. Being on a spectrum would have provided an explanation other than environment. As such, I'd obviously lied on the test.

"I didn't lie. There wasn't even a test, he just asked me a bunch of questions and showed me photos."
"Photos of what?"
"People's faces. I had to say if they were happy or sad."
"What questions did he ask?"
"I don't know, stuff about an old lady leaving an envelope of money on a park bench and a boy falling off his bike."
"What else?"

"Just stuff. Normal stuff about school and home and you."

"Us? What did he ask about us?"

"Just if you fight a lot."

"And what did you tell him?"

"That you fight a lot."

"Did you tell him about the time you laid on the bathroom floor naked and cracked eggs onto your penis?"

"No."

"Well there you go."

Technically I had lied; I stated that if an old lady left an envelope of money on a bench, I'd run after her and give it back. Maybe just knowing what the correct answer is counts though. There was mention of being retested a few months later, after I was caught shoplifting a cucumber, but my father said, "What's the point? He'll just blame it on us."

I don't know why I stole the cucumber. I just really liked cucumber sandwiches and was wearing a jacket with big pockets that day. I'd never seen my mother more mortified than the moment we were stopped by store detectives after leaving a supermarket. She cried in the car on the way home, and, after pulling into the driveway, said she didn't want my help carrying in the groceries. She also stated that mothers have to love their children, but that doesn't mean they have to like them.

It was an odd statement because we weren't the type of family that told each other we loved them. That was the last time my mother ever took me grocery shopping, which meant I didn't get to choose the breakfast cereal. Once she bought All-Bran.

I don't think I was tested for ADHD as it was considered more of a symptom of something rather than something itself. It's easy to self-test for it though: Simply attend a work seminar and, when a coworker named Walter offers you Adderall from a bottle he stole from his cousin, you accept. If you're then able to sit calmly and patiently through a 60-minute PowerPoint presentation about project management software, you may have ADHD. If you yell "Why are you doing this to us?" when shown a graph about graphs, are asked to leave, then drive your vehicle into a ravine, you probably don't have ADHD.

I saw Nathan at school a few days after the pool incident. He had stitches on the bridge of his nose and two black eyes that made him look like the Hamburglar - which is how he got his new nickname. The nickname didn't make any sense after his black eyes cleared up, but Hamburglar preferred it to his previous nickname (Funshine Bear) and, to keep it going, did a sneaky pantomime walk whenever anyone yelled, "Hey Hamburglar!" I was a bit annoyed by this.

Hamburglar and I didn't hang out again. I was partnered with Toby the wheelchair kid in science class, and Hamburglar was eventually expelled from school for trying to finger a student with down syndrome. I saw him working at a McDonald's several years later, which might be ironic if it weren't such a common job. You'd also have to be older than my offspring to get the irony if there was any.

"Seb, do you know who the Hamburglar is?"
"Is he a burglar who steals hamburgers? Lol."
"Yes."
"Wait. What? Why would he steal hamburgers?"
"Because he loves them. And he's a burglar."
"Risky crime for little reward. He'd be better off stealing something of value, selling it, and buying the burgers. Is this a real person or a character from something?"
"He's a McDonald's character. Like Mayor McCheese."
"Does Mayor McCheese steal cheese?"
"Why would Mayor McCheese need to steal cheese? His whole head is a cheeseburger."

To this day I can't swim under things, not even a floatie. It's like an aquatic version of claustrophobia. One of my worst fears is being trapped in some kind of cave or flooded building and having to swim through a tunnel to get out. Especially if the water is murky.

I won't even watch television shows that show people swimming under or through things. There's not a huge number of shows that feature this though, so it doesn't limit my viewing choices much. Also, as far as fears go, it's a relatively easy one to avoid. Some people are afraid of things they encounter every day; like colours, or knees, or numbers.

At least they claim they are; a fear of numbers seems kind of convenient. Particularly around tax time or splitting the bill at a restaurant.

"$43.75 each should cover it."
"Ah, I should have mentioned my arithmophobia."
"Sorry?"
"It's the fear of numbers. It's a real thing and I have it. As such, I'd prefer to pay my share of the bill with a haiku about foxes."
"That doesn't seem fair to everyone else."
"*Eyes glistening*
silent, creeping forward
chicken for dinner."
"That's not a even a proper haiku; haiku has a syllable-based 5-7-5 pattern. That was 4-6-5."
"Please stop."
"I'm going to need $43.75 from you, Gary."
"I feel attacked."

I probably shouldn't be so dismissive. My fear of swimming under things stemmed from past trauma, so it's possible someone with a fear of numbers was attacked by a 7.

Also, I gave Seb a diving knife for his tenth birthday. He wasn't as impressed as I thought he'd be but he wore it, strapped to his leg, in the shower. He tested the knife by cutting a bar of soap in half, then, while putting the knife back in its sheath, he missed and sliced open his leg. It wasn't a huge gash but it was flappy and bled a lot. I didn't have a Bandaid large enough for the wound, so I used toilet paper and duct tape. I didn't have Neosporin either, but sprayed the area with kitchen surface cleaner. The label claimed it killed 99.9% of germs but I don't know how accurate that statement is because his leg still got infected and he needed a tetanus shot and a course of antibiotics.

Caterpillar Legs

My parents subscribed to *National Geographic* when I was young. Each month, for three or four years, a yellow-bordered magazine was delivered to our mailbox inside a clear plastic cover. I wasn't allowed to open the plastic cover; I had to wait until my mother had read each issue and checked it for nipples. If and when she discovered nipples, she blacked them out with a thick Sharpie. I guess she thought I'd become a sex maniac if I saw a pygmy woman's nipples. I had my own nipples though, so I knew what they looked like.

This was well before the Internet was a thing. Nipples at the click of a mouse wasn't even a concept; computers were blinky panels in science fiction shows that warned the crew of approaching life forms or refused to open pod bay doors.

At one point, my parents also purchased an *Encyclopedia Britannica* set. It was thirty-two thick volumes and must have been expensive because they financed the purchase over two years. I think that was normal back then; an encyclopedia salesman actually came to our house and explained the financing and quoted statistics about children who grow up in households with *Encyclopedia Britannica* versus those who don't. It was completely up to my parents to decide if their children's future was worth sixty dollars per month - and if they'd regret the decision when my sister becomes a prostitute to pay for her next heroin fix and I'm in prison for mugging old ladies. Those weren't the salesman's exact words of course, but that was the implication. Additionally, if my parents signed up that day, they'd receive a mahogany-veneer bookcase to house their investment in at no extra cost. I don't think my parents gave too much of a fuck about their children's future, but they did care about giving the impression they gave a fuck, and it was a pretty nice bookcase.

The day the encyclopedias arrived - it took a few weeks for them to be delivered - we all flicked through them marveling at how we now had a world of knowledge at our fingertips. Then we never touched them again.

There were a few occasions when I'd ask my parents a question and be told, "Why don't you look it up in the *Encyclopedia Britannica*?" but it was a lot of effort. Nobody wanted to search through several volumes just to find out how springs are made or how many legs caterpillars have. Unless you're a spring manufacturer or insect scientist, they're questions that "I have no idea," and "Probably fifty," are perfectly fine answers for. It's six by the way; caterpillars have six legs. I honestly thought it would be a lot more but I just Googled it. They have ten other sticky-out things that look a lot like legs, but they're not actual legs, they're prolegs. The prolegs aid in walking and climbing though, so they're basically legs. It was probably an insect scientist who couldn't get past the whole 'insects have six legs' thing who called the extra ones prolegs.

"It clearly has more than six legs, Professor Plum."
"No, those extra ones are prolegs. They look like legs and work like legs, so I can see how you could make that mistake, but I'm an insect scientist."
"So which are the prolegs and which are the legs?"
"The extra legs are the prolegs."
"Yes, but which ones? The ones at the front?"
"Sure."

I also Googled how springs are made but I lost interest after the first sentence about alloys.

The *Encyclopedia Britannica* volumes collected dust until my friend, Wilson, came over to visit during school break. A few days before, my parents had purchased a new washing machine, and the cardboard box it came in was in our shed. Our old washing machine stopped working after my sister washed her Barbie Dream Camper in it.

I'm not sure if it was Wilson's idea or mine to turn the washing machine box into a computer, but I blamed Wilson afterwards.

The plan was to stick lights and switches on the box to make it look generally computerish. Then, and this was the clever part, one of us would sit inside the box with the *Encyclopedia Britannica* volumes and answer any questions that the person outside the box asked.

We started by gluing an entire roll of aluminium foil to the outside of the box. There were a lot of switches, knobs and light fittings in the shed, so we commandeered *all* of them and stuck them on. There was even a couple of taps and a golf-cart wheel. We also recorded ourselves making computer noises like 'beep beep boop' on a portable cassette player that the person inside could play while searching for answers. With hindsight, the finished product probably looked like a washing machine box with foil and junk glued to it, but at the time we felt we'd created something marvelous. Way too marvelous, in fact, not to share with the world.

We carried the computer down the driveway and set it up on the sidewalk in front of the house. Wilson then climbed inside while I stood at the curb holding a sign that read 'Ask the computer anything. 10 cents.'

A few cars slowed to have a look as they passed, but nobody stopped. Our only customer was Mrs Williams from next door who took a break from gardening to walk over and have a look. After heading home to get her purse and returning, she deposited 10 cents in the slot we'd cut out and asked, "What is 5 times 10?"

Wilson played the computer noise recording for a few seconds and then, in a robotic voice, answered, "FIFTY."

"You can ask it harder questions," I said, "they don't have to be math questions. The computer knows everything."

"Oh, okay, what is the population of Budapest?"

"No, you have to put another 10 cents in first."

"Oh, right... there you go. What is the population of Budapest?"

The computer noises went for a lot longer this time. At one point you could hear the tape rewinding and being replayed. Mrs Williams said she was happy to wait but I told her she could go home and I'd come and tell her the answer when the computer worked it out.

My father pulled into the driveway at that moment. There was no encouragement from him for our creativity and entrepreneurial skills; he yelled at us for taking Mrs William's money, embarrassing him in front of the neighbours, and for using his switches and knobs. He also told Wilson to go home and sent me to my room.

I watched, sadly from my bedroom window, as my father tore switches, knobs and taps off the box - ripping the foil in the process. You could tell the computer was just a cardboard box now; Mrs Williams would know it had been a ruse. I did wonder at the time why my father hadn't just carried the whole box back to the shed - it didn't occur to me that it was rubbish night.

The garbage truck came in the morning. The bins were emptied and the box was taken. I was watching cartoons in the living room, eating a bowl of Froot Loops, when my father walked in and asked, "Where the fuck are the *Encyclopedia Britannicas*?"

For the next five or six years, whenever I asked a question, any question, even something like, "What's for dinner?", my father would state, "I don't know, why don't you look it up in the *Encyclopedia Britannica*? Oh, that's right..." It wasn't clever, it was just annoying.

Forty years later, the last time I saw my father before he died from prostate cancer, I visited him in the hospital and sat by his bed watching the cricket. He was a bit out of it on pain killers, but still managed to say the *Encyclopedia Britannica* thing when I asked him what the score was.

Look At That Crema

Good luck if you're ever in Seattle and need to use a bathroom. There aren't any. The residents of Seattle just wade out into the bay and do their business while avoiding fishing vessels and orcas.

Businesses that do have facilities don't let anyone use them, not even Starbucks, because if they let one person, they have to let everyone, and then there's suddenly three-hundred homeless people pitching pop-up tents in the bathroom. There are a lot of homeless people in Seattle for some reason, you'd think they'd move somewhere sunnier. It's not like there's anything keeping them in Seattle; they don't have a house to sell or furniture to move.

If I were homeless, I'd move to Hawaii. If I'm going to sleep outside, I'd at least like a nice view and comfortable climate. I'd relax and swim during the day, and wander into beach luaus for a slice of rotisserie pig in the evenings. Larger luaus obviously, ones where an extra guest won't be noticed, not the ones with log seat circles and some dickhead playing a guitar.

The more touristy areas of Seattle, like Pike Place Market and the Space Needle, are kept relatively clear of pop-up tents, but venture just a few miles beyond the t-shirt and fridge magnet shops, and it's like a scout jamboree.

I'm not a fan of homeless people. I know you're not meant to say that, but they're annoying. No, I don't have spare change in my pocket, it's not 1985. I guess you're just meant to avoid eye contact and keep walking, but it feels weird pretending someone is invisible so I always end up giving them that nod where you lift your chin momentarily as if to say, "Hey." I'm not sure if the action has an actual name so I'm just going to call it a chinod. I'm aware of myself doing the chinod, and I don't want to, but it's like I'm programmed to.

The worst homeless people are the kind that hang out at traffic lights and stare at you when you pull up next to them. They're usually wearing a camo jacket and holding a bit of cardboard with 'anything helps' written on it. Well, I trust my chinod counts because that's all they're getting. If the sign also includes the words 'God bless', they're not even getting that. I'll just play with my stereo knobs.

I knew a homeless person once. His name was Jeremy and he wasn't homeless when I first knew him. We went to the same school but weren't in the same social group;

he was into football and I collected trilobite fossils. He was nice enough though; I was paired with him in gym class once and, when a couple of his sporty mates laughed at his misfortune, he said, "Don't worry about them, we're going to kick their arses." I don't remember what the activity was called but it involved a pommel horse, a medicine ball, and a bucket. Our gym teacher at the time was actually the art teacher, filling in for the regular gym teacher who was on leave for being a bit too touchy with the girls, so the activities were always bizarre. One of them included saying something you liked about another student before passing them a hockey stick with gold tinsel taped to it.

The only other interaction I recall having with Jeremy at school was during 'shot day'. I'm not sure how other countries did it, but in Australia during the eighties, kids received their vaccines at school. The vaccine being administered that day, I think it was for smallpox, wasn't administered by needle, it was air-injected and left a circular mark. It was more of a quick pressure than a jab. After receiving the vaccine and leaving the school nurse's office, I passed Jeremy waiting in line. His sporty mates were with him and one of them, a kid named Ethan, was saying stuff about the needle being the thickness of a straw and going three centimetres into your arm. Jeremy was pale and his brow and neck were beaded with sweat.

"Don't lie, Ethan," I said, "it's not even an injection, it's just air, and you hardly feel it." It was a passing comment, intended only to correct misinformation and belay fears, but Ethan took it as a personal affront and moved towards me with fists clenched. "You calling me a liar?" he asked. I had and I knew better than to do so; he was twice my size and had once thrown a book at a teacher. It could have quickly turned into a "meet me at the bike racks after school, I'm going to fucking kill you" situation, but Jeremy stepped between us and pushed him back stating, "You are a liar, Ethan, you haven't even gotten your shot yet so how the fuck would you know? Shut up and get back in line." And Ethan did.

I realise that wasn't a dramatic ending, but that's the point. Avoiding the "meet me at the bike racks after school" situation was my main focus at school. I'd been unable to avoid it only twice previously.

The first time was when I laughed at Patrick Cooper's answer to a history lesson question. The teacher asked what century the Industrial Revolution took place, and Patrick answered, "Swords." I'm not sure if he wasn't paying attention or somehow made a connection between blacksmithing and industry, but, at the time, I thought it was the funniest thing I'd ever heard; I cried and shook for several minutes, replaying it over in my head.

I was eventually told to leave the class and come back when I could control myself, and, as I walked out, Patrick said, "I'm going to get you after school."

He was waiting at the bike racks so I left through a side gate and walked home, leaving my bike at school overnight. Again, not a dramatic ending, but I wasn't going to be beaten up over a history question.

The second time was after I asked Sally Watts if she'd rather be a horse or a dolphin. In those days we didn't have normal covers on our school textbooks, our parents covered them in contact or wrapping paper to keep them from getting worn, and Sally's covers featured horses and dolphins. Sally stated that she'd rather be a dolphin, and I agreed that I too would rather be a dolphin. This was somehow construed - by Jason Kelly who had a thing for Sally - that I wanted to be a dolphin with her. I guess frolicking about in a lagoon together or something.

I emphatically denied this version of events and explained that I was simply agreeing that being a dolphin would be better than being a horse. Given the choice of animal, I'd actually be an otter. Jason wasn't having it though. It was one of those after-school fights where everyone somehow learns about it and turns up early to ensure a prime viewing position.

I'd gotten there earlier though and left already. The next day I wasn't so lucky. I did get out of class early again, but when I went to unlock my bike, I discovered someone had added their combination chain to my bike wheel. Panicking, I tried the trick where you pull the chain taught while turning the numbers to crack the code, but it was a six-number combination, not a four, and they're a lot harder to do. I considered leaving my bike and walking home, but the previous time I'd left my bike overnight at school, it had been stolen. I'd only had my new bike a couple of months and I doubted I'd get a replacement so soon; I'd have to ride my sister's bike to school, or worse, catch the bus. Only the poor kids and Toby the wheelchair kid caught the bus. The bell rang and I still had two numbers to go.

"Trying to undo my lock?" Jason asked. I looked up, startled. There were about ten kids behind him, more joined and a circle formed.

"I'm not going to fight you over dolphins, Jason."

"Why not, because you're scared?"

"No, because it's stupid. I don't even like dolphins."

"Then why were you asking my girlfriend about them?"

"I'm not your girlfriend," Sally said. She'd appeared with her group of her friends in the circle. "I don't like either of you. You've got pox all over your face and David whistles when he talks."

It was true, Jason did have pox all over his face. It looked like he'd been shot with hundreds of pellets from an airrifle. Some of the pox bled, others had what looked like spaghetti strands sticking out of them. Also, I was pretty sensitive about my whistle.

"Right," I stated, "I'm definitely not fighting now."
"Well, I'm still going to fight you," said Jason.
"What? Why? She just said she doesn't like you. No, you know what? Fine."

Adrenaline surged through my system. This was it; I was in a fight. Figuring it was best to throw the first and hopefully only punch, I swung at Jason's head - it was as if everything was in slow motion. It *was* in slow motion. Even as I threw the punch I thought, "Wow, that's slow." Jason stepped back, easily dodging my fist, he didn't even need to hurry. Though slow, my swing had momentum, and while most fighting stances list balance as the most important aspect, I'd gone for more of a 'mime pretending to climb a ladder' stance. My body twisted and I fell, striking my head on the bike rack with a solid 'dong'. It was hard enough to elicit a gasp from the crowd and to render me senseless for several seconds. I definitely had concussion because I remember touching my head, feeling that it was wet, and thinking I was at the pool. I managed to stand and apparently asked, "Where's my towel?"

I needed four stitches. There's still a spot on my head, at the front just above my hairline, where hair doesn't grow. I was off school for a week and my teacher sent me a big 'get well soon' card that was signed by the class. Sally drew a picture of dolphin under her message. I don't remember what the message said but the drawing was pretty bad. Especially considering she had pictures of dolphins on her textbook covers to go by. It looked more like a submarine with a face. Here's a quick re-creation:

While I don't recall much interaction with Jeremy, I passed him in the schoolyard regularly and we had a couple of classes together. He always gave me a chinod when we saw each other which was nice. A chinod may not seem like much, but there were only two other people at school that gave them to me and one of them was a janitor. The other was Toby the wheelchair kid and he didn't count because he gave everyone a chinod. You weren't allowed to have a problem with Toby even though he was a bit of a dick. Once, when we were playing the tinsel hockey stick game and it was his turn to say something nice about me, he said, "I like your dad's car." How is that about me?

Jeremy's family moved to a different suburb at one point and he changed schools. I barely gave it a thought at the time. The next time I saw Jeremy was ten years later, in 1996. I was living in inner-city Adelaide and walking down a street carrying a bag of milk. The milk was in cartons, in grocery bags, I didn't want you to get the idea I was just carrying a big bag of milk. I'd recently bought my very first espresso machine - one with knobs and steam nozzles to make lattes - and I'd underestimated how much milk I'd be churning through. At one point I was going through four or five cartons per day and gained about thirty pounds over the space of two weeks. I probably have strong bones though.

I eventually forced myself to cut back after a button on my favourite shirt popped off during a staff meeting. I was just out of university and working for a company called Lakewood Software Engineering. I was basically designing assembly line interfaces, but the pay was okay - enough to afford a small apartment in the city and buy an espresso machine. There were only twelve employees at the company and nine were young Asian programmers, all of them male apart from one girl. The girl was kind of cute, and I'd been working my way up to asking her out, but when my button popped off, she put a hand over her mouth, giggled, and said something in Asian. The other Asians laughed and one of them, a particularly annoying one with a bowl-cut who always argued with me about my interface designs, stated, "She says you've been eating too many hotdogs." The fuck? I don't even eat hotdogs.

Interface-issue guy and the girl eventually started dating but broke up because he yelled at her for slamming his car door or something. I could never really understand what was going on. I know she moved desks and interface-issue guy was moody for a few weeks. I think her name was Ping.

As I turned a corner, I noticed a homeless person in the doorway of an office building. He was sitting on a sleeping bag with his shoes off, rolling a cigarette. He glanced up from his task and we made eye contact. I gave him the chinod and he said, "David?"

"Jeremy?"
"Yeah. How have you been?"
"Good. What about yourself? What's it been, ten years?"
"Something like that."
"And you're homeless?"
"What?"
"Are you homeless? You know, the sleeping bag."
"Yeah, kind of. Just for a few nights though. I have a place planned."
"Well that's shit."

"Yeah. What's with all the milk?"

"Oh, it's for lattes. I bought an espresso machine and go through a lot of milk. Would you like one?"

"A carton of milk?"

"No, a latte. I'll make you one if you like and bring it back to you. I have disposable cups and only live around the corner."

You thought I was going to give him a place to stay, didn't you? That I'd invite him back to my place for a latte and then tell him he can crash on the couch for the night rather than sleep in a doorway. That would be pretty stupid though, to let someone you barely knew from high school sleep in your apartment. Someone you'd spoken to a total of maybe four times. It would be even stupider if, the next morning, you told him you had to leave for work but he was welcome to hang out for a bit and make something to eat before letting himself out. And that it was good seeing him again and you honestly wished him the best.

He stole my espresso machine.

I filed a police report but the officer I spoke to didn't inspire much hope of getting it back. I couldn't even remember Jeremy's last name. I'm not sure I ever knew it. The officer kept using the term 'valuable lesson' which was more annoying than helpful. For the next few years, whenever I saw a homeless person in a doorway or lying on the street, I did a double-take and looked them over to check whether it was Jeremy. I'm not sure what I would have done if one of them had been Jeremy, maybe yell at him for betraying our chinod-based friendship? Ask, "Where's my Gaggia Classic Pro, you thief?"

It's possible I'll receive a few derisive emails from coffee people for mentioning the Gaggia Classic Pro. "The Gaggia Classic Pro didnt exist in 1996," they'll type while touching themselves, "it was just called the Gaggia Classic back then, the Pro moniker wasn't added until 2019."

Coffee people can't help themselves. *Proper* coffee people that is, not the ones who buy hazelnut & hibiscus flavoured K-Cups. Proper coffee people weigh their beans. Did you know that? They weigh their beans on little electronic scales for fun. Proper coffee people poke, level, tamp, and preinfuse their meticulously measured grinds, chasing the perfect crema as if it's gold. "Look at that crema," they state, "it's beautiful." Also, proper coffee people pretend to hate Starbucks.

"It's not even real coffee. It's all the worst bits of coffee blended up and pressed into the shape of coffee beans. It's the coffee equivalent of chicken nuggets."

I'm a big fan of Starbucks. I don't care if it's chicken nugget coffee, it's coffee, and I plan all my outings around Starbucks locations. I figure if I have to leave the house, wherever I'm going has to be slightly less dreadful with a latte. Whenever I'm driving through town and see new retail construction, my first thought is, "I hope it's a Starbucks." Sometimes it is but usually it's a steakhouse; most of the people who live around here have owned a pig at some point. I understand some people have an issue with corporations like Starbucks driving out 'mom & pop' coffee shops, but if mom and pop don't have three stores within a five-mile radius of wherever I am at all times, maybe they need to reevaluate their business model.

"It's not looking good, Edith. We've only sold four coffees this month and are on the verge of bankruptcy. As such, I've decided to diversify our offerings by investing our remaining life-savings in fidget spinners."
"Fidget spinners?"
"Yes, they're very popular."

We even have a Starbucks sign in our kitchen. Several years back, when Starbucks changed their logo, I happened to be walking into a local Starbucks at the same time an old guy on a ladder was replacing the old sign with a new one. I asked what he was planning to do with the old sign and he replied, "None of your business."

I've no idea what his problem was. Sorry you have to climb a ladder and change signs for a living old man. Maybe you should have planned better for the future. Perhaps bought shares in Ford when the Model T was released. When I exited Starbucks, the old guy was at the top of the ladder giving the new sign a final buff. The old sign was lying on the ground. "Oi!" I said, and when the old guy looked down, I picked up the sign and ran.

As a Starbucks superfan, with all their albums and a poster in my room, it may come as a surprise that I had no idea the company started in Seattle. I mean, I may have read it somewhere, but it wasn't filed in the 'you might need this' section of my memory with Jenny's number and how to set the clock on a microwave we replaced in 2006.

It would be nice if we could organize our memories like files on a computer; deleting the painful or pointless memories and flagging the important ones. I'd probably just end with several hundred memories named 'qwqwerwqdsa' though.

"What's the Netflix password, David?"
"A photo of Seb with his top off at the lake, photoshopped to make his torso appear whiter than it really is."
"That can't be right."
"Hmm, try Dolan saying 'gooby pls'."

I realise *all* our memories, pleasant and horrid, make us who we are, but that's the point; I'd be a better me. One who knows how to do long division and read Morse code.

I definitely wouldn't be a graphic designer; with selective memory retention and dismissal, I'd have a cool job, like a park ranger. You'd be surprised how much park rangers have to learn, it's not all sitting in huts and telling people off. I wouldn't even have to work if I didn't want to, I could just spend the next ten years on *Jeopardy!* and retire a billionaire.

"And we welcome back our returning champion, David. It's his 2690th show and he's playing for ownership of Sony Studios. Good luck, David."
"Luck doesn't come into it, Kenneth. I am knowledge."

I don't actually watch *Jeopardy!* anymore. I stuck around for the guest hosts after Alex Trebec died but it was only to criticize. I'm not watching Kenneth host, he's the human equivalent of beige, and I can't stand old Blossom; I didn't pay an exorbitant amount for my 4K television to look at that. Who dresses her? Is she cosplaying Angela Lansbury? Also, shut the fuck up, old Blossom, nobody wants to hear your quip after every answer. We know you know the answers already and it's almost as annoying as your hair.

"The daguerreotype?"

"Correct. Invented by Louis Daguerre in 1839. Also, I don't just play a scientist on television, I have a philosophy degree in neuroscience with minors in Hebrew and Jewish studies."

"Wait, a philosophy degree? Do you have any peer-reviewed publications?"

"Yes, *Mayim's Vegan Table*, containing over 100 vegan recipes, is available on Amazon. And that takes us to a break."

I shouldn't belittle anyone's academic achievements. I'm sure old Blossom is a great neuroscientist. She probably spends her weekends in her shed working on a cure for Alzheimer's or Parkinson's disease when she's not out shopping in thrift stores for lightly-worn shoes.

"Hello, Michael J. Fox? This is old Blossom, I've discovered a cure for Parkinsons. The active ingredient is cat hair."

Honestly though, I have a silver swimming certificate from 1982 but that doesn't make me an expert on swimming pool Ph testing kits. Nobody's paying me to state, "I don't just play a chlorination professional in this commercial, I can swim." I would though, if the price was right. It would have to be at least five hundred dollars.

Everyone has a price and I know what I'm worth. I'd do a lot of things for five hundred dollars. Most of the things I want but don't buy are around that price. I'll be like, "Ooh, a drone, I'd like one of those," but then I'll see how much it costs and I know if I spend that much on something I want but don't *need*, Holly will organise an intervention.

"It's not an ambush, we're here to support you."
"Well I'm not participating."
"Yes you are, please get out of the inflatable spa."

It's a completely different story if it's Holly buying Lush products though. We should probably update our home insurance policy because Holly's side of the bathroom counter is worth more than the rest of the house.

The only thing Holly spends more on is travel. Not the actual travel part but the products required while travelling. I didn't even know a travel cupboard was a thing until I met Holly. Our travel cupboard contains thousands of miniature versions of everyday items, such as bodywash, cans of hairspray, and toothpaste, but also tiny plastic bottles and tiny bags to put the tiny bottles in. It has six drawers which are organised to match the human body - hair products at the top, then face, torso, groin, legs, and feet - and if you place anything in the wrong drawer or use an item, Holly knows. Any disruption to the system involves her emptying the travel cupboard, then putting everything back while taking inventory notes. It takes her about six hours and she has a special playlist for it on her phone.

"Three cotton buds are missing from the travel cupboard."
"So?"
"We've spoken about this. It's fine if you take things, just remember to email me a list of any items you use so I can add them to my travel cupboard Excel document."

I only need two products when I travel: underarm deodorant and hair stuff. Holly has a special suitcase for all the products she needs; it's a mini suitcase that fits inside a normal sized suitcase, but it's big enough to have wheels.

"Well, hopefully I won't need more than 997 cotton buds."
"We're going to Seattle for two days."
"And?"
"It just seems like a lot to pack for such a short trip. Do you really need eighteen different types of body lotion?"
"Yes, they're for different areas."
"You have eighteen different areas?"
"No, I have twenty. I packed my toe lotion and ear lotion in your bag because I ran out of room."

I only agreed to go to Seattle because I wanted a latte from the first Starbucks. I don't like the smell of fish markets and glass museums are more of a Holly thing. Located near the waterfront at 1912 Pike Place, the very first Starbucks would be easy to miss if it wasn't for the line outside. It has a modest front with peeling paint and the old brown logo - the one with the mermaid spreading her tails as if to say, "Hey sailor, get a load of this."

The best time to visit is half an hour before it opens, so around 6.30am. That way you'll be near the front of a line that stretches along the block, around a corner, and up a hill for half a mile. I'm not exaggerating, it's like the scene in the movie *2012* where everyone's waiting to get on the boat. We got there around 7am but it took us another half an hour to reach the end of the line. If I were homeless in Seattle, I'd get in the Starbucks line early and hold a sign saying, "Take my place for ten bucks." The closer you got to the front of the line, the more you could charge.

It's a statement on society that the line to get into Starbucks is longer than the lines to get into the Seattle Art Museum, Chihuly Garden and Glass, and the Olympic Sculpture Park combined. It's understandable though, I'll choose coffee over art every time. Less walking, etc. I'd definitely go to a lot more art museums if they rented ATVs to ride around on.

It's kind of like how Josh Gad has more Twitter followers than Clint Mansell. For those not familiar with Clint Mansell, he wrote the scores for *Requiem For a Dream*, *Pi*, *Black Swan*, *Doom*, *Sahara*, *The Fountain*, and *Ghost in the Shell*, and is one of the most talented composers in modern history. Josh Gad voiced a snowman in *Frozen*.

Holly and I were towards the back of the Starbucks line. I think we were in a suburb. After exhausting her list of all the things she'd rather be doing, Holly decided to wander off to do a bit of shopping while I kept our place. She popped back a few times over the next hour or so, to show me a fridge magnet and a wooden dog figurine she'd bought, then took a boat ride on the bay.

I considered giving up and leaving the line at one point, but then a family walked past with their Starbucks cups and the kid was holding a t-shirt with the original Starbucks logo on it. Besides, I was only about a block from the store by then; the time invested would become time wasted. As I shuffled slowly forward like the lever pullers in *Metropolis*, I reached a homeless guy sitting with his back to the wall. He looked up at me so I gave him the chinod.

"How you doing?" I asked. It looked like I was going to be standing next to him for a while.

"Good," he answered, brushing a matted strand of hair from his face, "I hate to ask, but do you have any change you might spare?"

"No," I replied, "my money is just zeros and ones on a computer somewhere."

"Fair enough."

"I'm not lying, I don't actually have any change."

"I believe you."

"I can buy you a coffee if that helps. Might have to wait a bit for it though."

"Okay, that would be nice."

"How do you have it?"

"Milky with lots of sugar."

"Easy, that's how like mine as well. Is the line always like this?"

"Yeah, it's crazy. It's not even the real first Starbucks."

"What? Yes it is."

"No, the first Starbucks was at 2000 Western Avenue. This is the second Starbucks. Look it up."

"I will…"

I looked it up on my phone and discovered he was correct.

"What the fuck? Why would they lie about something like that?"

"How long have you been standing in line?"

"Two hours."

"That's why they lie."

"Fuck this then," I said and left.

Still in need of coffee, I stopped at a bakery on my way to meet Holly. It was a small shopfront with tables and chairs outside and a Lavazza Coffee sticker on the window. An old Italian woman took my order for three lattes to go - I watched as she ground and tamped the beans then locked the portafilter into a Gaggia Classic Pro.

"Sugar?"

"Yes please, twelve in two and three in one. How long have you had that espresso machine?"

"The Gaggia? A couple of years."

"I had the same machine twenty-five years ago. I didn't even know they still made them."

"Of course they do," she smiled, pointing to shelves behind me, "We sell them."

This morning, Holly sat at our kitchen counter waiting patiently for her latte. She knows it takes about twenty minutes to make each one because there's a sequence of thirty switch and knob combinations to complete just to warm the machine up. It's worth it though. I held the shot glass of espresso up to the light and it lit up amber.

"Look at that crema," I said, "it's beautiful."

Wash Your Lettuce

Two of my coworkers, Walter and Ashley, have been dating for almost a year. If you'd asked me a year ago how long I thought their relationship would last, I would have said, "3pm, maybe an hour longer if Walter doesn't mention his telepathic tree theory or his groin rash."

Walter's telepathic tree theory is based on an incident that occurred while he was riding his bike home one night. It was dark and he was taking a shortcut through a park, when he heard the words, "Slow down!" He was startled by this, because there was nobody else around, so he peddled faster, turned a bend, and collided with a fallen branch lying across the path.

"And you've chosen to interpret this as a tree attempting to communicate telepathically with you?"
"There was nobody else around. And I heard it in my head, not my ears. Plus I have a plant at home that I take good care of."
"And your house plant told the park trees to keep an eye out for you while you're riding in the dark? There was

obviously someone else in the park and you just didn't see them."

"You're not a tree scientist."

There's a plant in the foyer and occasionally when Walter and I pass each other by it, I'll stop, pretend to listen to something the plant is saying, then state something like, "No! Walter did you really eat an entire tub of ice cream while watching *House of Dragons* last night?" It works best if I've overheard Walter telling someone what he did the night before. Also the plant being plastic adds a lot to the joke.

Ashley isn't our newest addition to the agency. We hired an assistant named Nicole in July, but she was also gone by July. I pride myself on my surliness but I was no match for Nicole's bipolar extremes; one minute smiling and helpful, the next glaring and whatever the opposite of helpful is. Unhelpful I suppose, but that doesn't convey just how unhelpful she was; it was like having a robot in the office - a stupid robot that has to be programmed to do each and every task and doesn't have a hard drive to save the information to so you have to program it again each time you want the task performed. It was quicker to just perform the task yourself.

Her resignation email was vaguely amusing though:

From: Nicole Kise
Date: Monday 11 July 2022 9.06am
To: All Staff
Subject: Resgination

To whom it may concern,

Unfortunately I don't feel that my career needs and expectations are being met at this company so I hereby formaly resign.

I need to work for a company that supports me and allows me to grow proffessionally instead of stifling my creativity and giving me no direction.

My last day of employment will be on Friday July 22nd 2022.

While I regret the circumstances under which I am leaving, I will work the next 2 weeks to ensure my duties are completed and that no unfinished tasks remain.

I am willing to make my departure as smooth and painless for everyone as possible.

Sincerely, Nicole Kise

From: David Thorne
Date: Monday 11 July 2022 9.17am
To: Nicole Kise
Subject: Re: Resgination

Nicole,

You don't have any duties or unfinished tasks. An unfinished task, by definition, implies a task was started. Sitting at your desk for the next two weeks glaring at us isn't a task.

Also, you spelled resignation wrong in the subject field and 'professionally' only has one f.

You will paid for the next two weeks regardless, but if you'd really like to make your departure as painless as possible for everyone, why not fuck off now?

All the best etc.

David

Graphic designers rarely date other graphic designers. They rarely even like each other. Interactions may be cordial at first, but eventually someone comments on a typeface or colour choice, and the next thing you know, qualifications, portfolios, and salaries are being compared. They'll apologise then do it again. In between spats they'll feign getting along but they're really hoping the other dies or at least fails spectacularly to impress a client with their shit logo design for a frozen yoghurt franchise.

There's very little 'team collaboration to produce the best outcome for clients', it's more like *Lord of the Flies* with Pantone swatches instead of pointy sticks. Our senior designer, Jodie, once threw a keyboard at me for suggesting Neue Haas Grotesk Display 75 Bold has a 'nicer feel' to it than Neue Helvetica 75 Bold. There were other suggestions between the initial suggestion and the attack, some to do with personal hygiene, but that just reinforces my point.

Walter and Ashley, however, get along ridiculously well. They're both good designers and, because they bounce ideas off each other without fear of ridicule or dismissal, their design work has improved over the last twelve months to the point where a project they worked on together was featured in *Creative Quarterly*. As such, they both received a wage increase for their efforts this week.

From: Walter Bowers
Date: Monday 1 August 2022 11.04am
To: David Thorne
Subject: pay

Did Mike tell you I was getting a raise? it only works out to $350 more every month but thats still good. Ashley got a raise to and Im going to ask her to move in with me.

....

From: David Thorne
Date: Monday 1 August 2022 11.15am
To: David Thorne
Subject: Re: pay

Walter,

Have you spoken to your plant about this? Do Ashley and the plant get along well?

It's a big decision but I figured you'd eventually move in with each other. Let me know what she says.

Also, don't forget we're flying to Asheville Wednesday. Melissa emailed you your boarding pass.

David

From: Walter Bowers
Date: Monday 1 August 2022 12.48pm
To: David Thorne
Subject: Re: Re: pay

she said no and we broke up

....

.

It wasn't that simple, it never is. Overexcitement creates a higher level of disappointment than standard excitement, and Walter overdoes everything.

"She probably thought you were going to propose."
"Why would I propose in the office kitchen?"
"Why would you get down on one knee to ask someone to move in with you? It doesn't make any sense."
"I was being romantic. I had a key in my pocket and everything."
"Wait, so you went down on one knee and then took a key out of your pocket to give to her? Please tell me this is what happened."
"She said we should have time apart and I asked if that meant we were breaking up and she said she didn't know. Which means we're breaking up, it always means that."
"Or she's just upset. Regardless, you should probably sort it out before Wednesday or it's going to be a miserable trip."

Asheville is small city in North Carolina. It's mainly known for its arts scene and historic architecture, but really there isn't much of either. Most of the 'art' shops feature tie-dyed yoga pantaloons, and I've seen old buildings before. It's a cute town though, nestled in the Blue Ridge Mountains, and our agency works with a marketing company based there. I'd usually go with Mike, our art director, but he forgot how stairs work last week and sprained an ankle. He has to wear a big boot if he leaves the house, so he doesn't.

Ashley and Walter worked on the project with me so it made sense to take them to the presentation. I'd like to say more about what the project is, but I signed a non-disclosure agreement in a room full of well-dressed lawyers. What I can say, is if your product poisons sixteen people, rebranding is a lot easier than convincing everyone it was a one-off thing and won't happen again. Also, always wash your lettuce before eating it.

Both Ashley and Walter were excited about the trip before Walter's kitchen proposal. Ashley hasn't had a 'vacation' in years, and Walter has never flown on a plane before. He has been in a helicopter, way back when we still rented them for aerial photography before drones took over, but the flight was cut short after just a few minutes and we were charged an exorbitant cleaning fee.

"Wait, so the agency pays for the flights there and back *and* the hotel room?"

"Yes, Walter, it's a business trip. Nobody would go if they had to pay for the flights and accommodation themselves. They'd go somewhere nice instead, somewhere without meetings."

"So it's like a vacation but everything's free except meals?"

"No, meals are covered."

"Oh my God. Everything's free? No wonder you and Mike go away all the time."

"Yes, I love business trips so much I could squeal."

Walter and Ashley have only spoken once since Monday and apparently the conversation ended with Walter retracting his offer for Ashley to move in and unfriending her on Facebook.

It's a little disappointing that their excitement for the trip has been tempered by a relationship hiccup. For them, not me; I see it as a kind of pantomime. Not a good one, if there is such a thing, but colourful and dramatic with a few entertaining moments. If nothing else, it might make the trip to Asheville more interesting - which is lucky because I have no ending to this story yet. As such, I intend to update the trip live from here on. That way we can experience the joy of travelling with coworkers together...

Update: Tuesday 10.15pm

Not exactly a travel update, but Walter just sent me a photo of a positive Covid test to get out of going. It's the same photo he sent me four months ago and when I called him out on it, he stated, "I didn't think you would scroll that far back up to check. Who does that?"

Wednesday 8.15am

The three of us are currently at the airport waiting to board. Our flight has been delayed which is lucky because Walter packed almost everything on the TSA 'banned from luggage' list apart from a gun and explosives.

Forced to discard a pocket-knife his father gave him and two gigantic 1000ml bottles of Redken shampoo and conditioner, Walter is blaming me for not informing him of the rules.

"How is it my fault, Walter? I'm sorry about your pocket knife but who packs that much shampoo and conditioner for a one-night trip? They looked like scuba tanks on the X-ray screen."
"I have dry to very dry hair."

Walter and Ashley haven't spoken a word to each other. The silence is a bit uncomfortable so I asked Ashley what she did last night and she stated she'd gone out to dinner with a friend. Walter appeared mortified by this so I pressed Ashley by asking, "A female friend or a male friend?" and she replied, "Just a friend," so she knows how to play the game.

Walter is now engrossed by something on his phone, attempting to give the appearance he doesn't care, but his face and ears are the colour of red peppers.

Wednesday 8.23am

Walter just asked what I'm typing and I told him it's a recipe for stuffed capsicums.

"What's a capsicum? Like the stars?"
"What?"
"You know, like 'you'll receive some good news concerning your finances this week.'"
"That's Capricorn, not capsicum. Capsicum is the Australian term for red peppers. Why would I be writing a recipe for stuffed Capricorns?"
"I don't know, it could be an Australian thing."

From: David Thorne
Date: Wednesday 3 August 2022 8.33am
To: Mike Campbell
Subject: Walter's knife

Mike,

Walter wasn't aware of TSA regulations and had to surrender his pocket knife. It was a gift from his father and he's rather upset about it. Is his dad dead? I can't remember. As this is a work trip, will the agency compensate him for the loss of a 'work tool' so he can replace it?

How's the ankle?

David

....

.

From: Mike Campbell
Date: Wednesday 3 August 2022 8.41am
To: David Thorne
Subject: Re: Walter's knife

David,

Walter should compensate us for putting up with his stupidity. His dad is definitely dead, we went to his funeral.

The ankle is what it is. I'm going to have carpet put on the stairs. Or a runner. Runners look nicer than carpet and are easier to change if I hate it. I'll just need to find nice mid-century modern stair runner rods. Do you know the ones I'm talking about? The brass ones.

Good luck with the presentation. Call me after it's over.

Mike

....

.

I do remember Walter's dad's funeral now. I'd been to a few others around the same time and they all tend to blend. They should have themed funerals to make them more memorable.

We hereby give notice that the service for Donald Robert Bower will be held at 10.30am on the 24th of April 2022 at Riverside Funeral Home. The theme is Pokémon.

All I recall from Walter's dad's funeral is that they served cocktail franks on coloured toothpicks. It struck me as odd at the time because the coloured ones are generally associated with more festive occasions, like children's birthday parties or Cinco de Mayo. Maybe they ran out of plain ones, sent a work-experience kid out to get more, and when he bought back coloured ones, it was too late to send him back again.

Wednesday 8.45am

I told Walter the agency will reimburse him for the cost of a replacement knife and he responded with, "Really? What about my shampoo and conditioner? Those big bottles aren't cheap."

We'd passed a Starbucks on the way to our gate so I told Walter that if he walked back to get me a latte, I'd replace his shampoo and conditioner. After he left, Ashley told me the Redken bottles cost $46 each. There's no way I'm spending $92 so it's lucky I said "replace" and not "replace with the same product." I don't care if he bitches, there's nothing wrong with Dial's 3 in 1 shampoo, conditioner, and car wax. Walter's absence also gave me a chance to pry further.

"So this friend you had dinner with last night."
"Yes?"
"When I asked if it was a female or male friend, why torment Walter by letting him assume it was male?"
"Because he's being an asshole. Besides, what makes you think it wasn't?"
"You wouldn't go out to dinner with a guy the day after Walter asked you to move in with him. Did you think he was proposing?"
"For a second."

"And were you pleased or horrified during that second?"

"I don't know. Both."

"He has a good heart and means well, he's just a bit oblivious sometimes."

"All the time."

"Right, he's coming back, let's pretend we're talking about stuffed peppers... so the trick is to bake the peppers empty before you stuff them, then stuff them and bake them again.

"You bake them twice?"

"Yes, nobody likes raw peppers. I generally use a creamy mushroom and broccoli risotto as the stuffing... oh, thank you, Walter."

"That's okay. Guess who I saw at Starbucks?"

"Ewan McGregor?"

"No, why would Ewan McGregor be at Starbucks? It was my old high school teacher, Mrs Bryant. She ordered a Frappuccino."

"Did you talk to her?"

"No."

"Seeing Ewan McGregor would have been better."

"Heaps better."

The lady at the boarding desk just announced they'll begin boarding shortly. As the three of us are seated together, I probably won't have the opportunity to update this until we arrive in Asheville...

Wednesday 8.56am

They've begun boarding but there's a wheelchair grandma in line so I have a few moments to add that Ashley just stated, "Oh, by the way, you should try the restaurant I went to last night - Zaytinya - they have the best Baba ghanoush I've ever tasted. My friend *Sarah* said the same thing."

Walter replied he thought baba ghanoush was what the Russian guys call John Wick, and Ashley responded, "You're so stupid."

So at least they're talking.

Wednesday 1.15pm

It's only a ninety-minute flight from D.C. to Asheville but it felt like ninety hours. Not really, I don't know why I wrote that, it did feel longer than ninety minutes though. Also, it's easy to state, "It's only a ninety-minute flight," but that doesn't include time spent getting to the airport, going through security, finding your gate, waiting to board, waiting to takeoff, waiting to get off the plane, finding your way out of the airport, and waiting for Walter to run back after he left his phone on the plane.

The airport at Asheville is about the size of a McDonald's restaurant, so it didn't take him long to go back through security, but they wouldn't let him back on the plane. I have no idea why, I guess it's just a plane thing we're not meant to question. I tried calling his phone a couple of times, hoping a flight attendant might answer so I could let her know Walter was heading back. On the third try, a deep male voice said something in another language and hung up. I tried calling again but the phone had been turned off.

"What language was it?"

"How would I know, Walter? It was another language."

"Did it sound French? You can tell when someone's speaking French even if you don't speak it. They say ooh a lot."

"I don't think it was French."

"Are you sure? There was a French guy on the flight. At least he looked French."

"It sounded more Mediterranean than French."

"The sea? Sea isn't a language."

"Or it may have been Arabic, one of the words sounded like static."

"Static?"

"Yes, it was something like, 'Ksshkssshhaaaa'."

"Oh my God, an Arab has my phone? Did you see any Arabs on the plane?"

"A few people had beards."

"I bet it was one of them. What am I going to do?"

"You'll just have to survive without a phone for 48 hours."

"How?"

It's a valid question. I don't know what I'd do if I had to go without a phone for that amount of time. Maybe I'd get a ton of work done; bathroom breaks would certainly be shorter and I wouldn't be distracted by videos of Indonesian men digging pools in a forest. I can't imagine getting into bed without a phone though, what do you do, just lie there? It's pointless even thinking about it however, as I've never lost a phone in my life. I did once leave my phone in a taxi but realised immediately and chased the taxi on foot for two blocks like the liquid-metal guy in *Terminator 2*.

I'm currently in my hotel room, sitting on the bed with my laptop on my knees. We have three hours before the presentation and I needed a break from Walter and Ashley. Nothing ever goes to plan though; Walter is sitting at the end of my bed, flicking through television channels and complaining about the sleeping arrangements. Melissa, our office manager, booked us adjoining rooms - one for me and the other for Walter and Ashley - before their breakup. Walter asked at the front desk for an additional room, but they're fully booked.

There's no way I'm sharing a bed with Walter, I sleep splayed. He can either sort things out with Ashley before tonight or sleep in a chair.

"I can't sleep in a chair. I'll be all crooked."
"Then sort it out with Ashley. You're stretching it out a bit."
"Stretching what out?"
"The whole 'I'm sad because Ashley doesn't want to share an apartment with me' thing. Just go back to the way you were before you asked her."
"I'm not going to pretend it's fine when it isn't. What would you do if Holly said she didn't want to live with you?"
"I'd wonder why it took her so long."

It's bound to happen eventually. I'm fully aware of my faults and mannerisms. I was once in a bad mood for a week because my favourite socks went missing. I never did find them. Now I'm in a bad mood again. The only logical reason I can think of why Holly hasn't left me yet is that she thinks I have money hidden somewhere and is waiting for the moment where I say, "Well done, you passed the test, I'm not really this dreadful, I just needed to know if you love me for who I am or are just in it for the money." Like that Elvis movie where he swaps his sports car for a motorbike and teaches watersports.

"Please, you don't have any money."

"Yes I do, Holly, it was all just a cunning ploy."

"You pretended to be broke for fourteen years?"

"A cunning and lengthy ploy. I was playing the long game."

"Where's this money hidden then?"

"It's in a sock in my sock drawer. A sock that I sometimes wear to give the impression that it's no different to any of my other socks. I put the money in a different sock when I wear the money sock."

"Are you talking about the fuzzy blue sock with four-hundred dollars in it?"

"Four-hundred and twenty-five dollars actually."

Holly isn't perfect either though; she puts paper towel rolls on the holder upside down. Nobody here is left-handed, we rip off paper towels with our right hand, not our left, our hands don't magically become ambidextrous when they're wet. Also, sometimes she buys the rolls with printed patterns on them. I can't do paper towel patterns; it changes the whole look of the kitchen. There's other things Holly does that annoy me, things not paper towel related, but, for the most part, I definitely got the better end of the deal.

"You definitely got the better end of the deal, Walter."

"With what?"

"With Ashley. She's way out of your league."

"What? No she's not."

"Of course she is. Your next girlfriend will probably have a cleft-lip or one leg shorter than the other. Ashley's next boyfriend will be a lawyer or an investment broker. A really good looking one who drives a Tesla."

"Riding a bike gives me good stomach muscles."

"He'll own a Peloton."

"Why are you even saying this?"

"Because you're being quite ridiculous. And because I'm not sharing a bed with you."

"I'll put a wall of pillows down the middle between us."

"Then I'll have even less room. I sleep splayed."

"What does that mean? Like a dog?"

"What? Splayed, not spayed. I sleep with my arms and legs splayed like I'm doing a jumping jack."

"Well, just don't."

"I have to, I have a thing about being constricted."

"What do you do when you're in a sleeping bag?"

"I don't sleep in sleeping bags."

"What about when you go camping?"

"I take a quilt."

"What if I sleep at the end of the bed, like horizontally?"

"How is that any better? I'm 6'3, Walter, where would I put my feet?"

"Your legs will be splayed so there'll be plenty of room. It's geometrics. Plus you could sit up a bit."

I do have a thing about being constricted. I can't even wear tight socks. When I was seven, my family was invited to a fondue party, and while my parents were outside mingling and dipping bread in hot cheese, two older boys rolled me up in a floor rug, wedged it in a corner, and left me there for over an hour. I cried the entire time and wet myself. When I was eventually rescued, I asked my parents why they hadn't looked for me, and they said they thought another kid at the party was me because we were both wearing yellow t-shirts. The hosts lent me a dry pair of pants to wear, but they were girls pants, so I spent the rest of the evening sitting in the car angry. I turned on the interior light so my parents could see me glaring.

Also, I do understand Walter staying annoyed to make a point, even if I'm not sure what that point is. I can stay annoyed at people for years just to make the vaguest of points - I once didn't speak to my friend Ross for three years because he tagged me in a bad photo on Facebook.

If someone does something that upsets you and you're only annoyed for a few minutes, what message does that send? Getting over it and moving on isn't a repercussion, it's permission to do it again. Say, for example, someone you know buys paper towel rolls with printed patterns on them, maybe of seahorses and starfish even though you don't live anywhere near a beach. You could simply state,

"Wow, what's the point of having a minimal kitchen aesthetic if you buy printed paper towels?" or you could refer to them during every conversation for the next month.

"Ahoy, can you pass me a paper towel featuring seahorses and starfish please?"
"They were out of plain ones. I told you that."
"It's fine, I like them. We should redo the entire kitchen in a marine theme. Maybe add a porthole."
"You do carry on a bit."
"Beach hair, don't care. Can you also pass me the peeler?"
'Where is it?"
"Starboard drawer."

In Australia, acting hurt or pouting is called 'being stroppy.' You can act stroppy or have a strop, as in, "Are you still having a strop about the photo on Facebook?" Walter took stroppy to a new level during the flight here. It looked like his bottom lip had been stung by a bee. Last week he was ecstatic about having the window seat, being that it was his first time on a plane, but he kept the window blind closed during takeoff to show us he was far too miserable to care about the view.

I sat in the middle seat, between Ashley and Walter, even though it wasn't our designated seating. I didn't mind as

I'm not a fan of the aisle seat; my legs don't fit behind the seat in front of me unless they're splayed, so whenever I have to sit in the aisle seat, I risk having a kneecap broken by the refreshments trolley. It's only ever happened to me once, but it was a solid hit, right in that little dip in the knee between bones that sends an electrical jolt up your spine and into your head. I was nodding off when it happened and screamed. I thought we were crashing.

Wednesday 2.30pm

I just asked Walter if he's planning to get changed soon, as the presentation is at 4pm, and he said, "Into what?"

His suitcase contains a pair of sneakers, socks, a red t-shirt with the Coca Cola logo on it, a pair of underpants, and a blue hoodie with what looks like a semen stain on the front.

"It's not semen, it's cappuccino froth, here smell it."
"I'm not smelling your hoodie stain. Why didn't you bring a shirt and jacket?"
"You said wear comfy clothes."
"For the plane. Is that what you were planning to wear to the presentation? Cargo shorts and a hoodie?"
"Nobody said it was dress up day."

'Dress up day' is a commonly used phrase at the agency to remind Walter to wear something other than cargo shorts and a t-shirt. Often when we take on new clients, they like to be given a guided tour of the agency. They poke their heads in doors and smile while Mike glares because you haven't fanned out your Pantone booklets dramatically. We're all meant to dress nicely and act professionally and say things like, "We're all really excited to be working on your project." Usually Mike does a walk-through before the client arrives to straightens pens and critique clothing, he even prepared scripts for us once but we refused to say them. The scripts were based on hearing Mike coming up the stairs with the clients, and were constructed to sound like everyone was busy and gets along well. I might actually add the email Mike sent so you can see how cringey it was for yourself:

From: Mike Campbell
Date: Monday 15 March 2021 11.32am
To: All Staff
Subject: Client impressions

Good morning,

The Gartner meeting is tomorrow at 9.30am. Please make sure your desks are clean before you leave tonight.

A couple of notes:

Melissa: Please smile when they come in. Nobody wants to see a sour expression that early. Show them into the boardroom and offer them coffee.

Walter: Don't forget it's dress up day. You'll have to go home and change if you do.

Ben and David: Try to act like you don't hate each other in the meeting. When one of you says something, the other should nod and say, "That's a valuable point!" or "That's valuable information!" and make a note of it.

Gary: When you hear us coming up the stairs, pretend you're on a call and say, "We won't have the final numbers until Friday, but early results show an 800% increase in sales. Yes, I'll let Mike and the team know how pleased you are."

Jodie and Ashley: Have the Reynold's annual report on the light bench. Act like you're both checking it carefully and say, "The spot varnish came out even better than expected!" and "The kerning is perfect!" Make sure there's a Pantone book fanned out and use words like pica and color seps.

Rebecca: Change the names on the scheduling board from KRS and Fusion Day Spa to Wendy's and Lockheed Martin just in case they look at it. And please don't wear your hair in a bun.

Kate: Enter the boardroom 5 minutes late and say something like, "I'm so sorry, I was on the phone with Scott from Hogan Lovells, they love the new logo by the way." and I'll nod and say, "I knew they would." and give you a fist bump.

Also, Jodie: Find photos of different kids online and print them out. Attractive kids, not your nephews and nieces. Put them on pinboards in people's offices to make it look like we have families.

Mike

....

I printed out a photo of a black baby and pinned it to my notice board, but Mike did a last-minute check of everyone's office and took it down. He also yelled at Walter for forgetting it was dress up day and made him hide in the bathroom while the client was there. Also, during the meeting, Ben stated, "My chair is a bit high but I can never remember which lever adjusts the height," and I said, "That's valuable information!" and wrote it down on my notepad. Mike looked annoyed and brushed my hand away when I tried to give him a fist bump.

I should also add that at the end of the meeting, when Mike showed the clients the studio, Gary messed up his lines and said, "Mike will be 800% pleased about those numbers on Friday."

For the next several weeks, whenever Mike stated he was pleased about anything, I asked, "Okay, but are you 800% pleased?" Some things don't require more than one person to find them hilarious. It's like when you see an ambulance rushing somewhere with its siren on and say, "They'll never sell any ice cream going that fast." Or maybe more like when you're picking someone up in your car and, as they go to open the passenger door, you drive forward a few feet.

I feel the driving forward thing is pretty much the pinnacle of humour. It never gets old despite the fact people have been doing it for centuries.

"Hop aboard my chariot, Thermometus."
"No, for you shall pull forward again and mock me."
"I swear on Apollo I shall not."
"Fine."
"HAHAHAHAHA."

Also, in case you were wondering how I came up with the name Thermometus, I asked Walter if he knew any Roman or Greek names, and he replied, "I don't know, Thermometer?"

Wednesday 3.15pm

Heading down to the foyer shortly as Ashley has booked an Uber for 3.30. She knocked on my door ten minutes ago and when Walter opened it, she asked, "Why haven't you changed yet?"

Walter explained that he didn't bring anything else so Ashley commandeered my suitcase and rifled through it looking for something for him to wear. He's currently sporting the pants and shirt I planned to wear tomorrow, which means I'll have to wear what I have on again. Also, I'm a lot taller and a bit wider than Walter, and he doesn't have a belt, so he kind of looks like he was shot with a shrink ray.

Ashley is currently doing Walter's hair in the bathroom; I heard her say, "Your hair is very dry today, are you leaving the conditioner in for five minutes?" and Walter replied, "Why would you care?"

Also, while Ashley was rifling through my suitcase, she asked, "Why did you bring rope?"

When I explained it was in case of a hotel fire, she said, "That's fine, you don't have to tell me if you don't want to." so I think she thinks it's a sexual thing.

Wednesday 5.30pm

The presentation went well. More often than not, when a marketing agency implements another agency's branding, something gets lost or misinterpreted in application; marketing people aren't designers and they almost always fuck up the size of the logo and the kerning and the grid and the negative space. I once told a marketing specialist she should be banned from ever touching Illustrator ever again and that if this were Brunei or Saudi Arabia, she'd have her hands cut off for crimes against design.

This wasn't the case today, however, as Walter and Ashley had worked closely with the marketing team on the project. The client was 800% pleased and signed off on the direction without changes.

I rang Mike after the presentation, in the Uber on the way back to the hotel, and told him the client hated the direction and wanted the brand name changed to Lettuce Rejoice. He heard Ashley laugh though so she ruined it. I had a whole thing scripted in my head about changing the logo to a lettuce wearing a halo, so that was wasted.

We agreed to meet the marketing team for dinner at 7.30 tonight; they're locals, so I have to trust their restaurant recommendation, but I would have preferred to eat pizza in bed. It's one of my favourite things to do when I travel, I've eaten pizza in bed in dozens of cities all over the world and base my favourite places on how good the pizza was. The best pizza I've ever had was in Sedona, Arizona. It had magic magnet powers. The worst was in Paris. I get that the French aren't known for their pizza, but whoever made mine had either never heard of pizza before that moment, or was really angry about something. It was just a blob of raw dough with half a tomato sitting in the middle.

If I could only ever eat one thing for the rest of my life, I'd definitely pick pizza. It's essentially whatever the fuck you want with bread.

"No, you have to pick one kind of pizza."
"You're not the hypothetical meal plan police. Fine, I'll have an 'everything' pizza and simply pick off the stuff I don't feel like eating that day. Just load it up with mangoes, spaghetti, cheesecake, soup etc. Maybe chips and dip."
"I'd pick sushi."
"Of course you would."

I don't eat fish because it smells like cat food. I can't even sit next to Holly when she orders fish in a restaurant. I can't sit across from her either, because she'd be breathing straight at me, so I sit at a different table.

Holly and Seb love sushi, so whenever we go to a Japanese restaurant, it's like they're on a date and I'm just some weird guy sitting at the next table staring at them while sniffing his salad. The salad is the only thing I can eat at sushi restaurants. I do like the vegetarian cucumber rolls, but I won't eat them because I know the guy who made them touched fish.

Ashley and Walter were extremely professional during the presentation; you wouldn't have known they were 'quarreling' unless you had some previous inclination or are one of those body language experts like you see on crime shows.

"Ah, did you catch that? The suspect scratched his ear. That's a dead giveaway he's either lying or has an itchy ear."
"Oh my god, it's like a special power. Tell me what colour I'm thinking of."

Also, one of the marketing people, a guy named Chase, casually flirted with Ashley and asked if she'd like to go for a drink after the presentation. Walter turned capsicum red again but didn't say a word. Ashley responded with, "Thank you for the offer but Walter and I are going clothes shopping before dinner. I forgot to remind him to pack a shirt and jacket."

Surprised, Walter added, "Yeah, this isn't my shirt or pants, they're David's. I don't usually wear old people's clothes." I gave Ashley the company credit card to use and told her to buy something for herself as well. There has to be small rewards for kindness, otherwise what's the point?

Wednesday 6.45pm

I should have put a limit on their spending but I was caught up in the whole kindness thing. Also, I assumed that with only an hour to shop, they'd be lucky to find one or two items that Walter liked. It must have been like the clothing store equivalent of *Supermarket Sweep* though, bolting down aisles grabbing everything off the racks.

Walter bought a $700 jacket, a shirt, a pair of pants, two pair of sunglasses, a belt, and a pair of leather business slippers. Ashley's $400 shoes brought the total to $1672.80. I'm equally outraged and in awe of their complete lack of restraint.

I'm going to have to use 'Code 300' with Melissa. It's the only way to avoid having the credit card charges questioned and Mike finding out. Basically, Code 300 means Melissa gets to spend around $300 on the company credit card, asks no questions, and combines our totals under 'office supplies'. It's not embezzlement if two employees are involved, it's procedure.

Wednesday 6.51 PM

Code 300 - $1672.80

Wednesday 6.53 PM

Awesome! I'm buying a popcorn machine.

I can't use Code 300 too often because it means having to subtly mention the high cost of office supplies whenever Mike is within earshot for a week or so.

"Gosh, does printer ink really cost that much? That's outrageous. It would be cheaper to buy a tank and stock it with squid, that way we'd never have to buy ink again; we could just startle them."

Walter is rather pleased with his new ensemble though; there's been a lot of poncing about in front of the mirror and he just declared, "I love business trips!" When I explained that he doesn't get a new wardrobe every trip, he nodded and said, "I should have bought *two* shirts. And a watch."

Walter also stated that while he and Ashley were shopping, he asked if she still loves him, and Ashley replied, "I'll always love you."

"And?"

"And nothing. The guy working at Sunglass Hut came over and interrupted us."

"They tend to do that."

"I know, right? Just fuck off and let me try on sunglasses."

"Did you inform him you were on a tight schedule and still had camping, snowboarding, and watersport outfits to buy?"

"No, I didn't know I could get camping stuff."

"Was it a 'I'll always love you and want to be with you,' or more of a, 'I'll always love you even when you're a distant memory and I'm with someone else'?"

"Hopefully the first one."

Wednesday 11.50pm

Okay, it's been a long day and a strange night. We had dinner at a restaurant called the Shanghai Dumpling House and it was as bad as it sounds. I don't trust dumplings and I'd rather eat Maggi packet noodle soup than pho. At least the packet soup has some flavour. I'm not sure who came up with pho but they should have kept it to themselves.

"So I take rice noodles and chopped veggies..."

"And cook them?"

"Kind of, I drop them in warm bone broth before serving."

"Right..."

"That's it."

"There's no flavouring?"

"It's tepid bone broth flavour."

"Okay, so it's basically the saddest soup imaginable. Is there at least bread to dip in it?"

"No."

The Shanghai Dumpling House also serves a type of tea called trà atisô. It's made from artichokes so the pho guy probably came up with that as well. Walter ordered it and described the taste as, "Kind of like when you lick a battery."

Walter sat to the left of Ashley and looked quite annoyed when Chase sat to her right. He asked if Ashley wanted to move closer to him, to make more room, then dragged her chair over with a loud screech before she had time to answer. She glared at him and Walter said, "What? Nobody wants to be scrunched."

There were only six of us, and nobody was scrunched, but I'm with Walter on this one. There was no need for Chase to sit next to Ashley; it meant I had to sit on the other side of the table, with the marketing director and his assistant, which required rotating my head to talk to them. I didn't give a fuck about talking to Chase and he didn't give a fuck about talking to anyone but Ashley. Mainly about himself.

Before the food came out, we knew what car he drove, his favourite music, his political views, and where he gets his hair cut. I asked Chase if it wouldn't be quicker to just send Ashley a PDF about himself and Walter laughed way too loudly. Chase seemed a tad miffed at being laughed at and asked Walter what kind of car he drives.

"I don't drive a car. I don't need to, I live in D.C."
"You catch a bus everywhere?"
"No, I ride my bike."
"What kind of bike do you own?"
"A Cannondale Habit."
"Nice. I own a Canyon Neuron CF 9, it cost a lot more than the Cannondale but has triple phase suspension and top tube protection. Do you ride, Ashley?"
"No."
"Well you look like you work out. Do you go to the gym?"
"No."
"I go regularly. I bench 280."
"Okay. Is that good?"
"Very. What do you bench, Walter?"
"Nothing. Because I don't have a tiny dick."

After a short but heated exchange, which included the phrases, "What's your problem, homo?" and, "Nice jacket, did you get it from Target?", the marketing director, a nice guy named Mitch, banged the table with his palm and said, "Enough, Chase."

"Yeah," Walter added, "Enough, Chase."

I probably should have also admonished Walter, but, to be honest, I was quite enjoying the show. Walter's head wobbles whenever he delivers what he feels is a zinger, as if to declare, "Checkmate motherfucker!" They're never zingers though, which is what makes it entertaining. The biggest wobble was after he responded to the jacket insult with, "No, it's from Tod Baker. Where'd you get yours, Target?"

Using the same insult doesn't warrant a wobble, and it's Ted, not Tod, so it was like the reverse of a zinger, but doubled, and too much for Chase to deconstruct and respond to with anything but, "What?"

Things calmed down a bit after that. Talk turned to work, as it does, and upcoming projects were discussed. At one point Walter and Chase even agreed on something, I think it was about broccoli. They'd both had a few beers by then; not enough to be besties, but enough to realise they'd acted unprofessionally. It had been a long day and Walter had lost his phone and Chase's dog had died a few days before, etc. When it was suggested we should get a drink somewhere before calling it a night, Mitch's assistant suggested a club close by called the Asheville Beauty Academy.

Mitch's assistant, Jake, is a level 8 gay. The scale goes from 'in denial' to 'dancing on a float in bottomless chaps'. One of my good friends, Kyle, has perfected level 5 gay to the point where you can't tell if he's gay or just really droll. After a few drinks he hits level 9 though; 'news anchor' Kyle becomes 'girl, let me tell you something' Kyle, and it's like an Easter egg hunt for cock.

"Tell me if I'm getting warmer!"
"You're getting colder."
"Are you sure?"
"Yes, Garth just likes the attention. He may have sucked a few cocks in his time, but only to make executive."

I'm not going to explain the above joke as it would also require an explanation of who Garth is, and nobody cares. Also, I'm currently annoyed with Kyle because he's moving for work. I only like about five people on the planet and they keep spreading out on it. It means the only local gay friends I will be left with are a couple of level 3s that live on a farm. Level 3 gays aren't fun, it's the 'I miss Seattle' level.

"The gay club?" Chase sneered.
"It's not a gay club," Jake replied, "It's an everyone club."

I feel I've covered Chase's personality enough to provide context for what happened at the club. More than enough really, some people are one-dimensional and Chase is practically a cardboard cutout. The best way I can think of to describe him physically, is that he looks like a can of Axe body spray that was turned into a real boy. Or maybe a car salesman - not one of the main salesmen, one of the salesmanettes that has to 'check with the boss' and comes back with a main salesman. Their shirt is always a size too small and their head a size too big. They also always have bad skin, like they shaved off dozens of pimples that morning, and thick eyebrows.

I don't usually describe people in my books, I mean you have no idea what Walter or Ashley look like apart from the images you've created in your head. Would it surprise you if I told you Walter is blonde? No? Fair enough. He isn't though so don't act smug. If I had to describe Walter's hair, I'd probably use the word buoyant.

Ashley is around 5"6, female, and likes cashews.

The Asheville Beauty Academy may seem like an odd name for a club, but it kind of works. The premises were an actual beauty academy in the 1950s, offering courses on hairstyling, makeup, and poise. It was originally owned by a pleasantly plump woman named Joyce from 1952 until 1957 when she lost her sight in a boiler explosion. I guess boilers just exploded in those days. The academy was then run by a woman named Gladys until she was murdered in 1959 by her husband for having a sexual relationship with a woman named Pearl. Apparently she was stabbed sixteen times with a pair of scissors and the husband was fined $270.34 - around 3K in today's money. The beauty academy then became a haberdashery, a book store, a dentist surgery, a florist, a jazz bar, and finally an 'everyone club'.

I like everyone clubs. They're friendlier and more welcoming than standard clubs. Standard clubs get sadder the later it gets, everyone clubs get more colourful. Maybe because drag queens take a long time to get ready and don't turn up until midnight. Not that I go to a lot of clubs; my bedtime is around 8.30 as I like a decent kip. There was a time when I used to stay up until 9.30, even 10, but the party animal thing eventually gets old. One day you're nodding along to *Always on My Mind* by the Pet Shop Boys while someone has a strobe light seizure next to you, the next you're nodding off during *Jeopardy*.

Time happens and probably will until we learn to harvest jellyfish DNA and turn it into a pill. We'll probably need to cure arthritis before that though. And Alzheimers. What's the point of living hundreds of years if you can't open a jam jar without a special tool or remember why you're standing in a warehouse holding a sword?

The club was packed and loud. The type of loud where you have to lean over the bar and yell into the bartender's ear to order. Mitch had paid for dinner so I opened a tab and Chase took full advantage of it. He ordered four rounds of tequila shots and downed several vodka and Red Bulls within the first hour. I don't do shots but I did have a couple of vodka and Red Bulls - which is probably why I'm still awake and writing at 1.30am. Adrenalin may also have something to do with it.

Mitch called it a night before 11 and said his farewells. It was a work night and he had an early meeting the next day. I was also ready to leave, as we have an early flight, but Ashley and Walter were having fun so I ordered another round of drinks. Shortly after, the DJ played a track called *Do It To It* and Ashley squealed with delight and tried to drag Walter onto the dance floor. Walter declined so Ashley headed to the dance floor without him. At this point the sequence of events gets a bit messy, as it was crowded and people were coming and going from our table, but Chase also headed to the dance floor after throwing back another vodka and Red Bull. A few minutes later, Ashley returned to the table, looking upset, and asked, "Can we go?"

"Are you okay?" asked Walter.
"Yes, I just want to go," replied Ashley, collecting her bag and putting it over her shoulder.
Chase appeared behind her and grabbed her arm, "You don't want to dance with me anymore?" he sneered.
Ashley looked at me pleadingly, "Please can we go? Now?"
"Of course," I nodded, "What's going on?"
"She's being a fucking tease," Chase said.

Walter punched Chase. I've never seen him show even the slightest hint of violence in all the years we've worked together, so it was a bit of a shock. It was definitely more of a shock to Chase though. It was a solid punch, to the chin, and I think Chase's mouth was open when it landed as I heard his teeth clack shut like a belt being snapped, even above the sound of the music.

Chase staggered backwards, flailing, but managed to stay standing. Walter punched him again. This time it was face on, not from the side, and Chase went down. Prone, but with his head propped up against a table leg, Chase spat out a gob of blood and a tooth came with it.

A big black guy wearing a shirt with SECURITY written across it appeared and put his arms out as if to say, "What the fuck is going on?" Ashley pointed to Chase and said, "He put his hand up my dress."

"Do you want to press charges?" the black guy asked.

"No," replied Ashley," I just want to leave."

Chase started to climb to his feet and the black guy put a boot on his chest and pushed him back down.

"Okay," the black guy said to Ashley, "you have a good night, miss, I'll take care of this."

Walter and Ashley waited for me outside while I closed the tab. I looked back at Chase, still on the ground with a boot on his chest as I left. He was yelling something at the black guy, I'm not sure what, and the black guy reached down and slapped him hard.

Ashley had her head on Walters chest and his arms were wrapped around her. We walked back to the hotel and they held hands the whole way. Walter had to use his left hand as his right hand looks like it's broken; I asked him if it hurts and he said, "Yes, but it was worth it."

Walter came into my room but only to grab his stuff. I'm happy about this because I wouldn't have made him sleep in the chair. It's currently 2.05am and I'm going to write a quick email then crash as I have to be up in four hours.

From: David Thorne
Date: Thursday 4 August 2022 2.15am
To: Mitch Sanders
Subject: Chase

Good morning Mitch,

I was going to call you in the morning but I know you have an early meeting.

Firstly, I value our working relationship and feel we share the same desire to produce quality work. The Jasper and Aarke projects are excellent examples of this and I hope to collaborate on many more projects in the future. I will chat with Mike Friday about the Moen account as I want you to be part of it.

Secondly, we will not work with Chase Allen.

After you left tonight, Chase sexually assaulted Ashley and a physical altercation followed. You may notice Chase is missing a tooth.

As such, it will be a provision of future collaborations that Chase plays no part in any project associated with Wyndham Miller & Associates.

I will give you a call after our flight to discuss.

Regards, David

David, effective immediately, Chase Allen is no longer an employee at this agency. Please give my apologies to Ashley and let her know I feel terrible about this. Have a safe flight. Call me whenever you get a moment. I'm cancelling my morning appointment. Mitch

Thursday 7am

All I care about when I wake up is coffee. There's a coffee machine in my room but when I turned it on it buzzed for several seconds and then caught fire. I have hundreds of tiny black wiggly things floating about the room now. I assume they're burnt plastic so I'm probably breathing in pure carcinogens. I had to catch the world's slowest elevator to the hotel restaurant to get coffee and I was so pissed off about it I said to an old lady, "Is it?" when she said, "Good morning."

I grabbed four coffees in takeaway cups at the restaurant; two for me and one each to take to Ashley and Walter. I have no idea how they take them, so I just made them the same way I like mine; extra milk and lots of sugar. They were both awake and packing when I tapped on their door. Ashley said, "Aww," when I handed her a coffee, which is all the appreciation anyone needs. Walter took a sip of his and said, "Fuck, that's good!" which was slightly disappointing as I was hoping I'd end up with three. They were both surprisingly chipper for the early hour.

"Are you doing alright?" I asked Ashley.

"Yes, very alright," she beamed.

"We're moving in together," added Walter, also beaming.

"Of course you are. Oh, by the way, Mitch is firing Chase this morning."

"Really?" asked Ashley.

"Yes, I spoke to him during the twenty-minute ride in the elevator to get coffees. It's effective immediately so you won't have to deal with Chase again. How's your hand, Walter?"

"Good," he replied, holding up his right hand. It was purple and huge like an inflated latex glove.

"Oh my god!"

"I know, pretty cool huh?"

Ashley took a sip of her coffee and asked, "How many sugars are in this?"

"Twelve."

"Twelve?"

"It's a big cup."

Also, Walter asked me what was on my face and when I looked in the mirror, I discovered I had a black smudge under my nose. Apparently when the tiny black wiggly floaty things land on you and you rub them, they leave a smear. I'd ridden the elevator and ordered coffees with a little Hitler moustache. I need to shower before we leave for the airport. As such, I'm calling it for Asheville unless something noteworthy happens between now and when we get back to D.C.

Thursday 8.20am

Okay, not overly noteworthy but I told Walter about 'First Class Counter Passes' - the process where the lady behind the counter prints first class seat passes if any become available and places them on the counter for anyone who wants them.

"Are you serious?"
"Yes, it's part of their standby upgrade service."
"Why wouldn't everyone want them?"
"They do, that's why that guy over there is standing near the counter. First to grab the passes gets them."

It's not a thing, and there's no first class on our flight because it's a puddle jumper, but Walter is currently standing a few feet from the counter, watching both the guy standing near him and the lady behind the counter like a hawk. It's given him something to do apart from complain about not having his phone.

Ashley shook her head and said, "He really is stupid."

"Yes, he is. Was it the 'knight in shining armour' thing last night that made you change your mind?"

"About moving in? No, it was when he hugged me outside the club. His heart was beating fast and he was shaking."

"Well, I'm happy for you two. The last few days have been far less entertaining than I'd hoped they'd be. I actually took notes the whole time, hoping to get a story out of it, but it's hardly an epic tale of love and adventure."

"I did get a nice pair of shoes out of it."

"That's true. And a grope."

Thursday 8.32am

Walter sat down and said, "Fuck you're a liar." Apparently the lady behind the counter placed a handful of pink luggage tags on the counter and Walter grabbed them.

Thursday 1.30pm

The flight itself was mostly uneventful; Walter left the window blind open and Ashley nibbled cashews out of a sad little sandwich bag. I don't think Walter's hand is broken because there was a moment during the flight where we hit a bit of turbulence and Ashley squeezed it without Walter passing out. He just did a stretchy face thing like he was being pulled into a black hole.

I ended up in the aisle seat but it was an exit row so I had plenty of leg room. Also, when the flight attendant asked the mandatory exit row questions about being able to assist with evacuation in case of an emergency, Walter told her that he's quick and an excellent swimmer.

'Why would you tell the flight attendant that you're an excellent swimmer?"
"I am."
"Okay, but why tell the flight attendant that?"
"In case we crash in the water."
"It's an inland flight, we don't fly over the ocean."
"There's rivers and lakes. And ponds."
"That's true. If we crash in someone's pond, you could swim to the edge and grab a net. What about puddles? Are you an excellent puddle swimmer?"

Ashley gave me hug when we said goodbye at the airport. It was kind of odd but hugs are always nice. I asked Walter if he also wanted a hug and he said, "No, I haven't forgotten about the puddle comment."

"Really, Walter?"
"Yes, I meant big ponds. With ducks."

About the Author

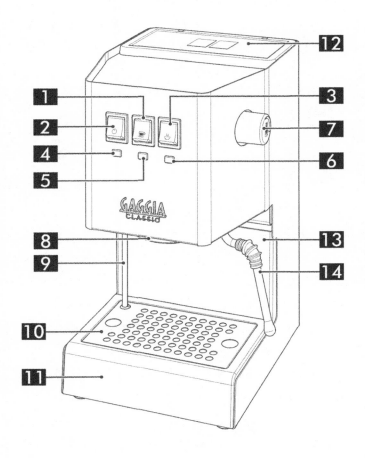

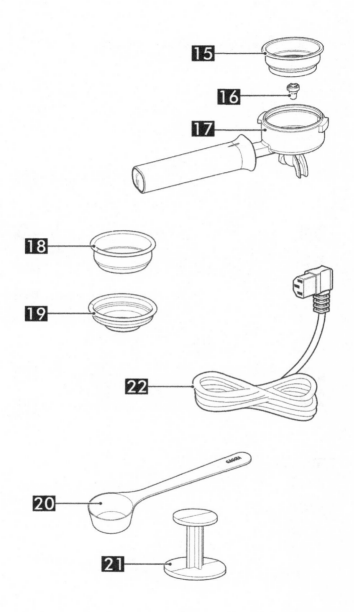

PART IDENTIFICATION

1 Switch 2

2 Switch 1

3 Switch 3

4 Switch 1 light

5 Switch 2 light

6 Switch 3 light

7 Knob

8 Thing the water comes out of

9 Drain pipe

10 Grill

11 Ew tray

12 Lid

13 Water tank (removable)

14 Third degree burn pipe

15 Small hole bean juice thing for 1 and 2 cups*

16 The thing you lost on day one

17 Twister handle thing

18 Bean juice thing for 2 cups

19 Bean juice thing for 1 cup

20 Weird long handled spoon

21 Coffee squasher

22 Power snake

* For use with pre-ground beans only.

INSTALLATION

1. Remove the lid or water tank and fill with cold water up to the MAX level.

2. Insert the power snake into the outlet at the back of the machine and the other end of the power snake into a wall socket with suitable voltage.

3. Press switch 1.

LOADING THE CIRCUIT

1. Place an empty cup under the thing the water comes out of without inserting the twister handle thing and press switch 2. You should hear the sound of the pump and after a few seconds water will start to come out of the thing the water comes out of.

2. After filling the cup, press switch 2 again.

Note. If water does not come out of the thing the water comes out of, continue as follows:

1. Place a cup under the third degree burn pipe and turn the knob counter-clockwise.

2. Press switch 2 to activate pump. After a few seconds, water will start coming out.

3. Close the knob and try again.

TWISTER HANDLE THING PREHEATING

1. Insert the empty twister handle thing into the thing the water comes out of with a 45° movement to the left and turn it right to lock it in place.

2. Press switch 2. After approximately half a cup of water has been dispensed, press switch 2 again and wait a few minutes for the machine to reach the correct temperature with the twister handle thing inserted.

BREWING COFFEE

1. Remove the preheated twister handle thing and fill the bean juice thing with the required amount of ground coffee. A tablespoon of coffee for each shot is standard.

2. Squash the coffee with the coffee squasher, pressing evenly to obtain a flat surface. Remove any coffee residue from the edge of the twister handle thing and the bean juice thing.

3. Insert the twister handle thing into the thing the water comes out of with a 45° movement to the left and turn it to the right to lock it in place. The twister handle thing handle should be perpendicular to the machine.

4. Wait until the switch 2 light turns on then press switch 2. Once the required amount of coffee has been dispensed, press switch 2.

USING THE THIRD DEGREE BURN PIPE

We recommend using fresh whole milk at a cold temperature. The density of the frothed milk will depend on the milk fat content.

1. Press switch 3.

2. After 30 seconds, or when the switch 3 light comes on, turn the knob slightly counter-clockwise to eliminate any condensation from the third degree burn pipe and then close the knob again.

3. Place a jug, half-filled with cold milk, under the third degree burn pipe.

4. Place the third degree burn pipe nozzle just below the surface of the milk.

5. Turn the knob counter-clockwise to let steam come out.

Note. To froth the milk correctly, the third degree burn pipe nozzle must always be in contact with the milk and not with the froth. Once the desired frothing has been achieved, the third degree burn pipe nozzle should be pushed down further to heat the milk well.

6. Once the desired result has been achieved, close the knob by turning it clockwise to stop dispensing steam. Pour the milk into the coffee.

7. Press switch 3.

DISPENSING HOT WATER

1. Press switch 2 and wait a few minutes until the switch 2 light turns on.

2. Place a cup under the third degree burn pipe.

3. Slowly turn the knob counter-clockwise and press switch 2 and switch 3 at the same time to allow for hot water to be dispensed.

4. Once the desired amount of hot water has been dispensed, stop dispensing by pressing switch 2 and switch 3 and turning the knob clockwise.

CLEANING AND MAINTENANCE

Regular cleaning and maintenance will keep the machine in perfect condition and ensure perfect coffee flavour, a constant coffee flow, and excellent milk froth for a long period of time.

Cleaning the third degree burn pipe

1. After each milk frothing, clean the third degree burn pipe with a damp cloth.

2. Turn the knob counter-clockwise, allowing the steam to escape for one or two seconds to clear the third degree burn pipe nozzle hole.

Cleaning the twister handle thing

The twister handle thing should be kept clean to guarantee perfect results. Every day, remove the twister handle thing from the thing the water comes out of and wash it with warm water. If you notice a malfunction when brewing, immerse the twister handle thing in boiling water for 10 minutes, then rinse.

Cleaning the grill and ew tray

Remove the ew tray and the grill and wash them with water. Do not use abrasive cleaning tools.

Cleaning the water tank

Remove the water tank and wash it with fresh water. To remove the water tank, first remove the ew tray and then remove the drain pipe by pulling it downwards.

Note. When reinserting the tank, make sure that the silicone tubes are inside the tank and that they are neither twisted nor blocked.

Cleaning the thing water comes out of

Regularly remove any residual coffee grounds from the thing the water comes out of and rinse with hot water by pressing switch 2 for 10 seconds without the twister handle thing attached.

DESCALING

Limescale builds up with the use of the appliance. We recommend using Gaggia Decalcifier Descaler Solution to descale it. Never use gravel as this will affect the performance of the machine.

Note: Descaling should be performed once a month.

1. Insert the twister handle thing into the thing the water comes out of and turn it from left to right until it locks into place.

2. Remove and empty the water tank. Pour half the contents of the descaling solution into the water tank and fill it with fresh water up to the max level.

3. Press switch 1.

4. Dispense half the water in the tank from the third degree burn pipe, and the other half through the thing the water comes out of.

5. Repeat the process.

6. Rinse the water tank and fill it with fresh drinking water.

7. Dispense half the water in the tank from the third degree burn pipe, and the other half through the thing the water comes out of.

8. Repeat steps 6 and 7 if you can be bothered.

THINGS TO KNOW

1. Espresso machines require a finely ground coffee bean blend. Ideally, the coffee beans should be ground just before use. It is preferable to use a grinder mill rather than a blade mill because the latter releases too much coffee powder and produces an irregularly ground blend. Never use kidney beans in place of coffee beans.

2. Dispensing steam continuously for more than 60 seconds will empty the boiler and damage the unit. If this occurs, return the machine to the place of purchase and say it stopped working for no reason.

3. The machine is equipped with a manual energy saving function. After 20 minutes of inactivity, please switch the machine off.

4. The steam function is ready to use after 30 seconds even if switch 3 isn't illuminated. Using this method will cause an increase in the amount of steam. Or an explosion.

4. The third degree burn pipe gets hot during and after use. To avoid burns, have someone else clean or adjust it for you.

5. To prepare another coffee immediately after using the steam function, lower the boiler temperature by dispensing hot water from the coffee brew unit before use. Otherwise the coffee will taste like burnt pasta.

TROUBLESHOOTING

Problem:	Solution:
Not brewing	Turn machine on.
	Ensure there is water in the tank.
	Make sure the twister handle thing is not clogged.
Brews fast / no crema	Ensure the grind isn't too coarse.
	Check the coffee has been squashed properly using the coffee squasher.
	Ensure the twister handle thing is in the thing the water comes out of.
Noisy pump	It just is.
Cold coffee	Wait for the switch 2 light to come on.
	Preheat the twister handle thing.
	Drink faster.
Not frothing	Check the third degree burn pipe is not clogged, missing, or inserted too deep in the milk.
On fire	You left switch 3 on, didn't you?

Woah. That's a big QR-code.

Made in United States
North Haven, CT
01 January 2023

30482482R00146